Latch Hook

Heidi Gustad

LEISURE ARTS, INC. • Maumelle, Arkansas

Table of Contents

Welcome to Latch Hook

Rainbow Wall Hanging (Heidi Gustad, 2018)

Latch hook might not be the first craft that comes to mind when you think of colorful, contemporary and cutting edge. For many of us, latch hook feels exclusively linked to crafting kits of the past, featuring scenes with mushrooms, clown faces and branded characters. I was perfectly ambivalent about latch hook for years myself, writing it off as dated, played out and childish. That is until a few years ago when I found myself with the overwhelming urge to create something usable with a decades-old stash of yarn ends that encompassed every color, fiber and yarn weight under the sun. Cracking open my needlecraft encyclopedias, I learned how to latch hook and quickly started knotting away with my scrap stash on a few pieces of canvas. By the time I finished experimenting with pooling similar colors into ad hoc gradients and shapes, I had created a gorgeous, four-pane wall hanging that felt like my grandmothers' patchwork quilts but cooler. I was in love—I had discovered a yarn craft that was faster, funkier, and a much more fun way to create artistic pieces for my home.

Do you want to try it too? This book includes 12 patterns that range from square one, beginner-friendly projects to those with more complicated finishing techniques. If you're new to latch hook, this is the place to be! The learning curve is delightfully shallow for getting started and you can begin your first project as soon as you learn to make a single latch hook knot.

This book opens with a step-by-step guide to latch hook basics, followed by tutorials to teach you finishing, binding, trimming, backing and hanging techniques to give your latch hook projects a professional finish. With this book, I'm hoping to share just a few of the wide range of fun things that can be made with latch hook and arm you with the skills to take the craft even further on your own.

Yours in yarn,
Heidi

Getting Started

Latch hook is great because you only need two special supplies, both of which are affordable: rug canvas and a latch hook tool. The rest of the supplies you need are all standard craft room staples: yarn, a tapestry (yarn) needle, safety pins, a sewing needle and thread, Tacky Glue®, a ruler, scrap cardboard, and a couple good pairs of scissors, one for heavier duty cutting and one for precisely trimming yarn. I recommend reading through everything from this point in the book through the first project to familiarize yourself with techniques and terminology before you begin your first latch hook project.

Rug Canvas

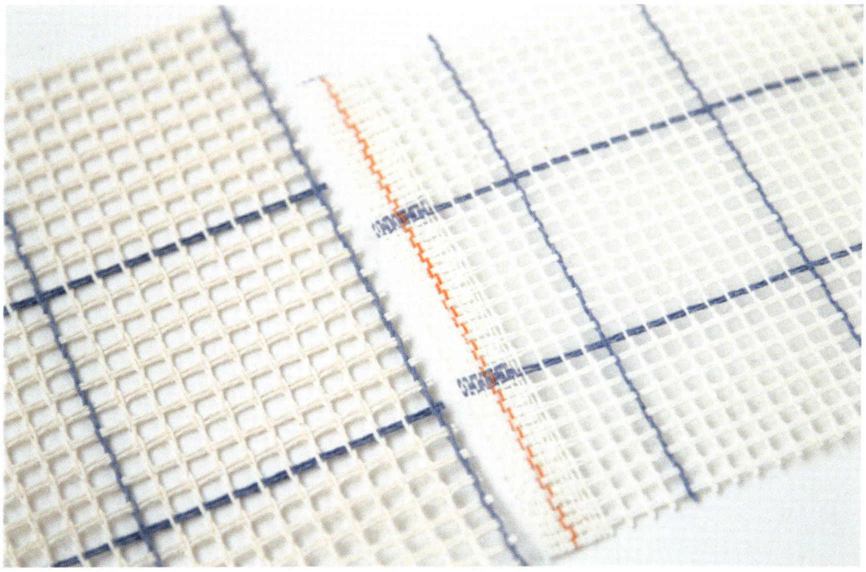

What to Know about Rug Canvas

Rug canvas is the woven grid of sturdy fabric onto which knots are tied to form latch hook designs. There is a lot more to mesh rug canvas than meets the eye! Rug canvas is primarily available in two sizes: 3.75 mesh and 5 mesh. 3.75 mesh rug canvas features 4 squares per inch, and 5 mesh canvas clocks in at 5 squares per inch. The difference may sound subtle, but as you'll see throughout this book, yarn weight and knot density (whether you're working with 4 or 5 knots per inch and how many strands of yarn you work per knot) can make a huge difference in how a project turns out.

Fig. 1

Fig. 2

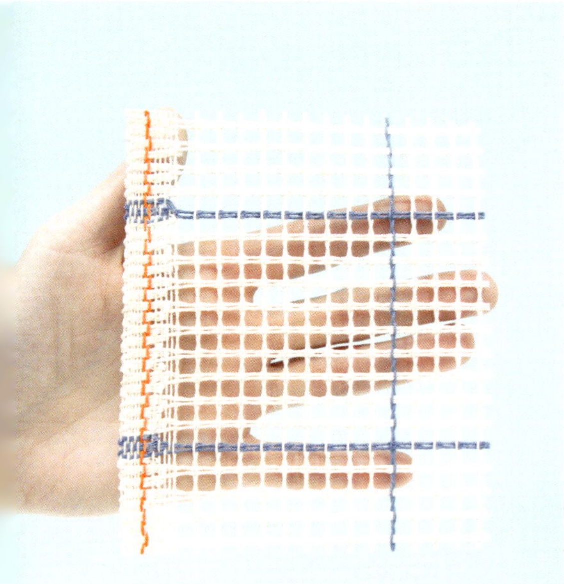

In latch hook, there's a right direction and a wrong direction to consider when beginning your project. Grab a piece of rug canvas and look at the grid of strings in front of you. Two strands of thread are woven vertically and horizontally in each direction. When hooking a latch hook project, the vertical strands should be twisted around each other, intersecting between each pair of horizontal strands, which simply run parallel to each other **(Fig. 1)**. As you hook, you will be working your knot around a pair of horizontal strands. The twisted, vertical strands add structure to the canvas itself and ultimately your finished latch hook projects, so they should be left bare.

Most brands of rug canvas come with the tenth vertical and horizontal set of strands woven in another color **(Fig. 2)**. This helps makers keep track of their location as they work a project, and I recommend using canvas that employs this clever feature whenever you latch hook. It aids in both counting knots and following charts, which comes in handy when working more complicated projects.

How to Calculate Rug Canvas Size

In latch hook you need to leave some unworked canvas beyond the outside edges of your project, called seam allowance. The rule of thumb to follow for seam allowance in latch hook is to leave at least an inch, though for beginners I recommend a full 2" of seam allowance on all sides to be safe. For the purposes of this book, we are using 2" of seam allowance for most projects.

Example: Your finished project is 9" x 9". You will add 2" of seam allowance on all four sides. So, your canvas piece should be 13" x 13".

You may elect to incorporate more than the pattern-recommended seam allowance depending on the project. For projects that don't have square corners, the rug canvas sizes provided in each pattern include seam allowance starting from the widest point of the design, so there may be more than 2" of seam allowance at some points in your canvas to begin with. Unnecessary canvas can be trimmed during the project finishing stage at your discretion.

Struggling with Fraying Canvas Edges as You Work?

Not all latch hookers have an issue with fraying, but if you find you're struggling with the raw edge of your canvas fraying as you knot, you can secure your raw canvas edges with masking or packing tape. Note: If you use tape, it has to be carefully removed before any sort of finishing can be accomplished.

Yarn

As discussed, latch hook projects are created by knotting small lengths of yarn to your canvas. Strand length, number of strands per knot, number of knots per inch, and area of your finished project must all be considered when contemplating yarn for a latch hook project. This will help you determine how much yarn a given latch hook project requires to complete. *As this is a beginner book, all project instructions include fully calculated project yardage and strand length. Yardage calculation instructions are included so that you can use this information to make a latch hook project without the use of a pattern once you master the basics.*

Vocabulary

- **Pile length** means how far from the rug canvas your work measures; approximately how tall it would be if laid flat on the floor.
- Used alone or held together, **strands** are the small pieces of yarn used to tie individual latch hook knots.
- **Yardage** refers to how much yarn (in yards) a given project requires. The number of yards per skein is listed on commercial yarn labels for the makers' reference.

How to Calculate Project Yardage

There is a useful formula for planning a latch hook project from scratch. It will help you determine how long your yarn strands have to be to create a certain pile length, as well as how much yarn you're going to need to hook & finish an entire project. When buying yarn for any yarn craft, be it knitting or latch hook, be sure to get enough yarn of the same dye lot to complete all of a given latch hook project.

Pile Length

The first thing you need to determine is your pile length (see definition above). For a rug with a 1" pile, strands that measure 2½" are required. Why? Because in latch hook, yarn strands are folded in half and secured to the canvas with a knot, which takes approximately ½" of yarn to make. Once you know your pile length, you can calculate your strand length.

Strand Length Formula

(Pile length x 2) + ½" = strand length

Working with More Than One Strand at a Time

Some projects call for the use of more than 1 strand of yarn per knot. Before calculating yardage or hooking a project, confirm the number of strands of yarn per knot called for in your project. If you're working with two strands for instance, your project yardage will double (not counting additional yarn for finishing and binding).

Yardage Calculation Formula

(Number of knots per inch x number of strands per knot x strand length x area of project in square inches) = total inches needed for project. Then to calculate yardage, divide total inches by 36" to determine the number of yards needed for your project before finishing and binding (see finishing & binding guides, pages 10 & 12).

For example: Let's say your finished project is a 4" x 4" square worked with a 2" pile length with yarn strands held double on a piece of 3.75 mesh canvas. How much yarn will you need to hook this project?

Answer: 4 knots per inch x 2 strands per knot x 4½" strand length x (4 x 4 square inch project area) = 4 x 2 x 4½ x 16 = 576" of yarn

- 576" divided by 36" per yard = 16 yards.
- Sixteen yards will be required for the knotted portion of the project. Additional yardage will be required for finishing and binding.

Cutting Your Yarn

If you have made a latch hook project from a kit, chances are you're used to working with machine cut yarn strands that arrive in little bundles wrapped in plastic. (They kind of look like hay bales.) For a more accessible take on latch hook, all of the projects in this book have been designed with yarns common to major craft stores. You will cut your own yarn strands for all of the projects in this book, which will enable you to latch hook with any yarn, including repurposed yarn.

Supplies needed: scrap cardboard, marker, ruler, scissors, string, and project yarn.

Measure and cut your cardboard to the appropriate size (strand length). If you wish, you may also mark measurements on the cardboard at this time for reference. Working in small amounts, wrap yarn around cardboard without working too tightly. When you've got a thick, even distribution of yarn wrapped around your cardboard, tie each side with string **(Fig. 3)**. (Pro tip: Using string that's cotton or a different fiber than your strand yarn makes bundling individual strands easier.) Cut along each end of your cardboard ruler **(Fig. 4)** to form two bundles of yarn strands **(Fig. 5)**.

For projects that require a lot of yardage, the yarn cutting process can grow tiresome using the cardboard method. However, there are a range of commercially available yarn measuring and cutting tools if you're looking to add to your craft toolbox. In particular, most tassel makers work beautifully in the place of scrap cardboard for cutting latch hook yarn.

Note: If a single project calls for more than one strand length, you will need to repeat the cutting process using additional cardboard cut to another size.

Fig. 3

Fig. 4

Fig. 5

How to Latch Hook

When it comes down to it, most of your time on a latch hooking project will be spent tying hundreds of small knots to form a design, which is why getting your first project started is so fast compared to many other needlecrafts.

A **latch hook tool** consists of a handle with a metal rod coming out of it called a shank that is often bent for ease of use. At the end of the shank is a latching mechanism that aids in the knot creation process. When properly functioning, your latch should have a free range of motion, opening and closing without resistance.

How to Tie a Latch Hook Knot

Supplies required: latch hook tool, rug canvas, yarn cut into small strands

1. Take a strand of pre-cut yarn and fold it exactly in half around the shank of your latch hook tool, between the latch and handle **(Fig. 6)**.

Fig. 6

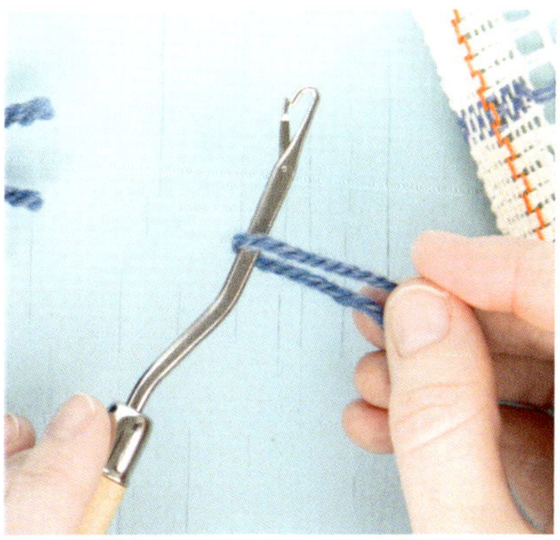

2. Holding the tails of your yarn in one hand, use the other to insert the closed tip of your latch hook tool under a set of horizontal (NOT twisted) strands of your rug canvas and bring it back up to the front side of your canvas **(Fig. 7)**.

Fig. 7

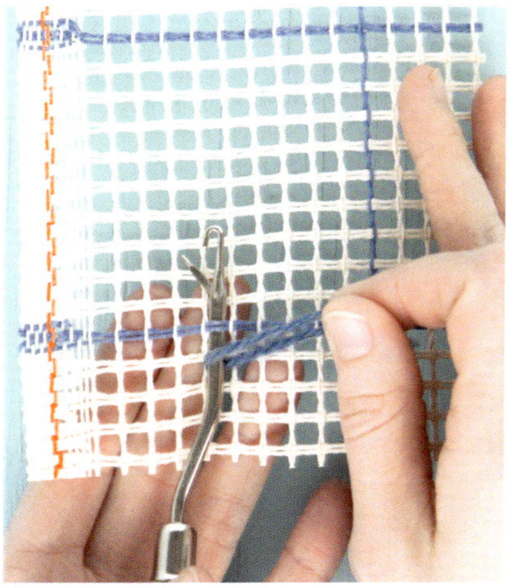

3. Wrap the tails of your yarn around the shank, inside the closeable area of the latch hook tool **(Fig. 8)**.

Fig. 8

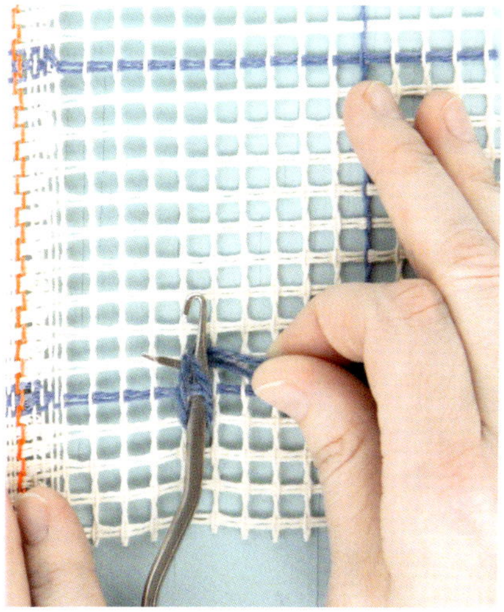

4. Draw the latch hook tool back under the horizontal canvas strands, closing your latch and catching the yarn tails wrapped around the shank **(Fig. 9)**.

Fig. 9

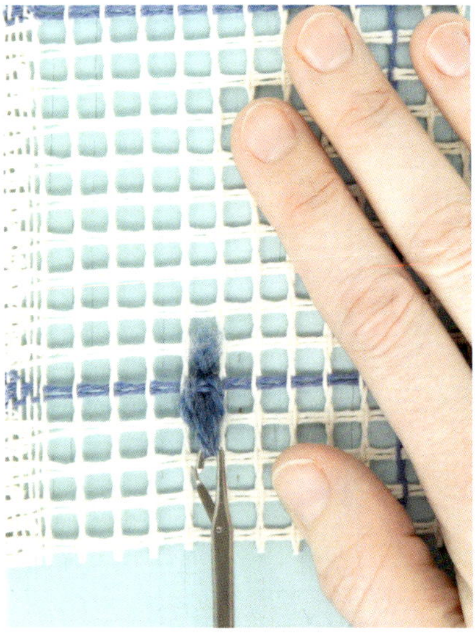

5. As you continue to pull, your latch hook knot will be formed, and the tool and yarn will no longer be touching **(Fig. 10)**.

Fig. 10

6. To secure your knot, gently tug on the tails of your yarn **(Fig. 11)**. This is also a great opportunity to confirm your tails are even and your yarn didn't split.

Fig. 11

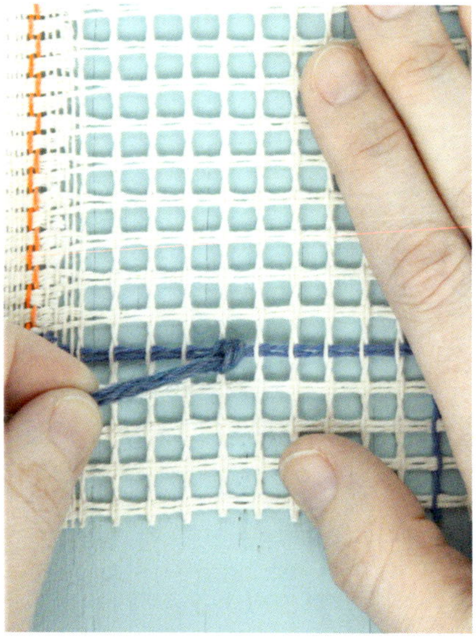

Working with multiple strands per knot: You can work a single latch hook knot while holding as many strands of yarn as you like and your canvas will allow. I usually max out at 3 strands, but if you want to recycle some lace or fingering weight yarn from your stash, you could experiment with even more. All you do is hold more than one strand at a time as you latch each knot—the trick being two or three times as many tails to wrangle.

Practice: If you're a first time or first-time-in-a-long-time latch hooker, I suggest grabbing a canvas scrap to practice your technique until you've got the muscle memory down **(Fig. 12)**. Just make a small square and call it a coaster if you're not a fan of making swatches for the sake of technique. Your finished projects will look significantly better the more you practice your skills, I promise!

Fig. 12

Reading Patterns & Charts

For folks coming to latch hook with a background in kits, you might recall a sort of paint-by-number situation, with designs printed right on the canvas you knotted on. That doesn't really work with a book. In many needlecrafts, gridded charts are used to let makers know where different colors and/or stitches should be used to create a given design, whether that be a sweater, cross-stitch sampler or latch hook project. In this book, the color of each square on a gridded chart indicates where on your gridded canvas to knot a certain color of yarn.

Most patterns in this book are worked from a combination of chart as well as written instructions, beginning with a list of supplies needed and project setup information. Before working a pattern, read it in its entirely, including taking a look at the chart. Gather your supplies and cut yarn strands as directed in your pattern with the technique demonstrated in the Yarn section (page 5).

Working From a Chart

Patterns in this book begin with project setup information. Then, those with charts instruct makers to, "Start your project centered on the canvas, leaving a minimum of 2" all around. Knot the design following the chart provided." For the purposes of latch hook, this simply means remembering to knot your first knot far enough from the edge of the canvas that you still have seam allowance. Do not start your project without seam allowance. It will fall apart. (See the Rug Canvas section, page 3, to learn about seam allowance and why it matters.) The location of all other knots is relative to the first in any latch hook project. To avoid errors, some makers prefer to mark their seam allowance with permanent marker for extra peace of mind. You can start wherever you prefer, but in latch hook, it's recommended to work across each row of a chart horizontally, one at a time from bottom to top, to produce the most even finished results.

Keeping Track of Your Work & Working from a Split Chart

In this book, larger scale projects with charts have been split up into sections. The approach to tracking your location in a given chart is up to you. Modern makers swear by everything from a sticky note to scanning charts into apps designed for following charted patterns. You may also use permanent marker, contrasting scrap yarn or safety pins to mark where on your rug canvas your chart(s) begin and end, particularly when working from a split chart. When working from a split chart, remember that seam allowance is only required around the outside edges of your project, not each individual chart.

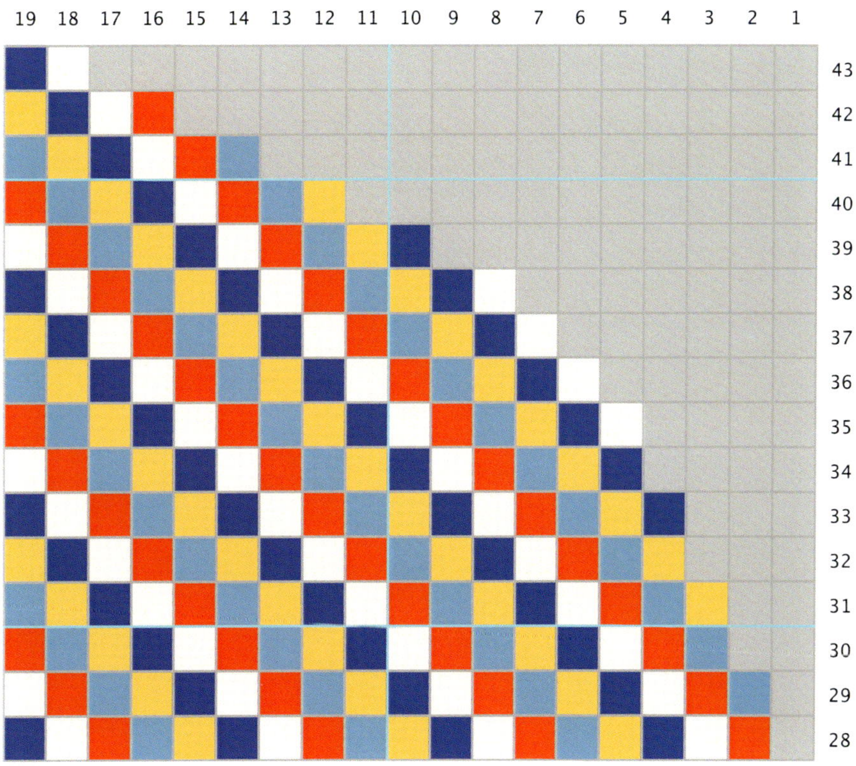

Finishing Guide

Throughout these introductory guides to latch hook, you've been reading a lot about seam allowance, the excess canvas beyond where the knotted portion of your work ends. At some point, project seam allowance needs to be folded to the back of your work and secured in place with hand stitching or knotting. For the purposes of this book, this is called "finishing." Finishing is quite literally straightforward for square-edged projects, but for those that are not, the process is a bit more abstract.

Finishing Supplies: rug canvas scraps, sewing clamps or clothespins, scissors, tapestry (yarn) needle, yarn

First, Trim Your Canvas (optional)

With all finishing, the first step is to trim any excess canvas to your preferred length if needed. All canvas dimensions in this book are given with 2" of seam allowance incorporated on all sides.

For smaller projects, you may prefer to reduce unnecessary bulk by trimming your seam allowance to 1"–1½", however, seam allowance under 1" is not generally advisable in latch hook as it may result in compromised non-seam allowance canvas.

Square Finishing (ONLY for projects with square corners)

Square finishing is straightforward in latch hook. Trim your seam allowance as desired, then fold the unhooked canvas to the back of your work, lining up your grid to avoid a twisted edge. Working through two canvas layers at once, simply knot your project as if you were knotting a single layer. If your canvas is slipping out of place, employing sewing clamps or clothespins is helpful.

In square latch hook finishing, there will always be a small rectangle of unnecessary canvas at each corner. Simply cut out or fold under the unnecessary piece of canvas at each corner of your project as shown before finishing its perpendicular edge (**Figs. 13 &14**).

Fig. 13

Fig. 14

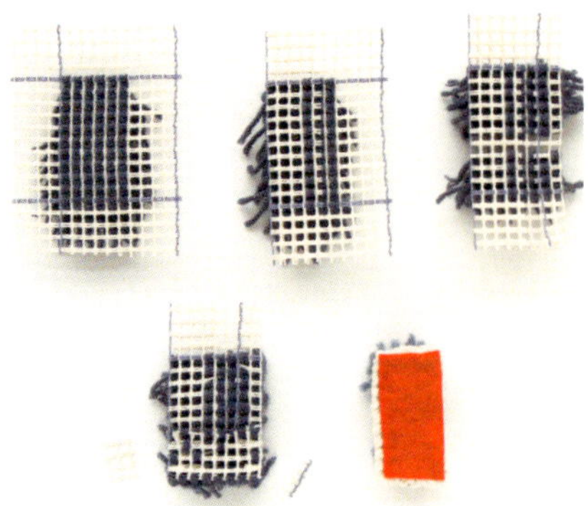

Non-Square Finishing

Non-square finishing is a little more abstract of a process. Just like with square finishing, begin by trimming seam allowance as desired (**Fig. 15**).

Fig. 15

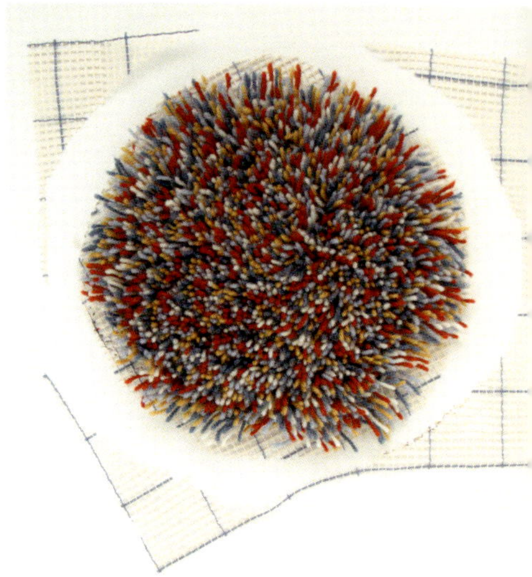

Unlike with a square edge, you don't have to align canvas squares to effectively finish the edge. You simply fold your seam allowance to the back of your work **(Fig. 16)** and stitch it in place by hand. It doesn't have to be pretty, just secure.

Fig. 16

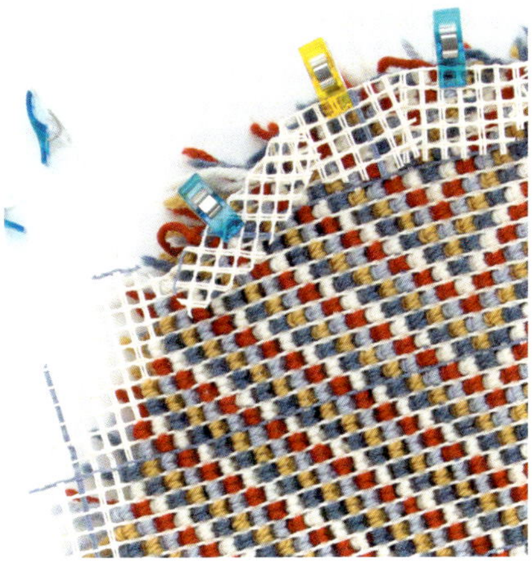

As you fold back your seam allowance, natural folds of excess canvas will form due to working on a curved edge. Carefully cut the canvas where it's fluting before layering the edges over each other and stitching them in place. As you work, selectively snip and remove canvas that proves to be unnecessary **(Figs. 17 - 18)**.

Fig. 17

Finishing FAQ

I made a square project and forgot to finish it with square finishing!

Square projects don't HAVE to be finished with square finishing, but square finishing is generally less time consuming than non-square finishing. Every maker has their own style, but you should use whichever method suits the task at hand.

If you forget to finish as you go, you may hand finish your project with non-square finishing. Or you can opt to use the square finishing method after the fact, tearing out and re-knotting appropriate knots.

Reinforcing Rug Canvas During Finishing (optional)

Some latch hook projects are big and heavy! Over time, extra big projects, heavy projects, and projects that experience a lot of use show signs of wear and tear like anything else. But reinforcing with canvas extends their longevity

Fig. 18

Projects that especially benefit from reinforcement are those with a long pile like the Layered Heart Tote (page 31) and the Fried Egg Wall Hanging (page 57). Patching in extra canvas around and/or behind the heart and "yolk" knots helps the canvas stretch less under the weight of the project as it hangs.

Projects with lots of curved edges like the Faux Shearling Throw (page 48) also benefit from reinforcement. You can patch in scraps or even large panels of canvas to the back of your work to reinforce areas that look like they'll need it.

To patch in extra pieces of canvas, simply locate or cut a patch of rug canvas to your desired size. Working with the same size canvas (3.75 or 5 mesh) as your project is preferable. Whether you're incorporating a patch at the center of your project or along a curved edge, you simply place your patch on the back of your work and hand stitch it in place with a tapestry needle **(Fig. 19)**.

Fig. 19

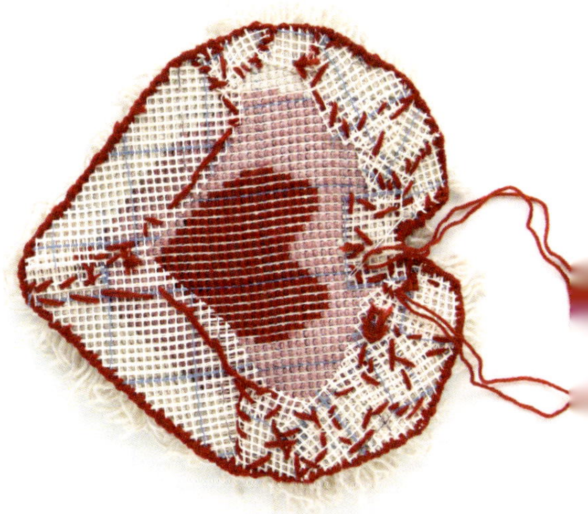

Binding Guide

In quilting, binding is the process makers use to finish the raw edge of a quilt, preventing fraying and securing layers together. In latch hook, binding refers to finishing the raw canvas edge. For the purposes of instruction, finishing and binding have been separated into distinct processes in this book, and the binding process can vary a lot from project to project (or be skipped entirely). When binding occurs in latch hook, it is done after finishing a project's rug canvas. Latch hook binding is done to hide and reinforce the folded canvas edges and prop up yarn strands at the edge of a project **(Figs. 20 & 21)** .

Fig. 20

Fig. 21

As with many things in latch hook, there are exceptions to these best practices. Projects such as the Faux Shearling Throw (page 48) are bound and backed in one fell swoop with stitching. More on project backing can be found in Backing and Hanging Guide (Page 15).

How to Bind Latch Hook Edges

Depending on the latch hook project, you will use hand sewing, specifically Whipstitch or Blanket Stitch, to bind a project's edges. Whipstitch is a bit simpler to work, but sometimes Blanket Stitch is needed to cover raw edges better than Whipstitch can.

Whipstitch

Whether you're stitching around a folded edge or joining two pieces of canvas, line up the canvas to begin, holding work in place with sewing clamps as needed. Secure the tail of your working yarn to your canvas. Bring the needle through both layers of canvas and draw tail through **(Fig. 22)**.

Fig. 22

Working in the same direction, insert the needle a short distance from the previous stitch and draw tail through **(Fig. 23)**. Repeat this process to finish your raw canvas edge, securing with a knot.

Fig. 23

Blanket Stitch

Line up the canvas to begin, holding work in place with sewing clamps as needed. Working with the back of your project facing you, secure the tail of your yarn to the canvas.

Insert your needle from the back to the front of your project and draw the tail all the way through **(Fig. 24)**.

Fig. 24

Placing your needle in the same hole, insert it from front to back and draw through. Bring the needle sideways through the loop you just created and pull up to gently tighten **(Fig. 25)**.

Fig. 25

A finished and bound non-square latch hook project edge from the back.

Particularly for non-square projects, binding is your opportunity to secure edges like this to avoid fraying.

With the back side of your work facing you, insert the needle slightly to the right of your first stich **(Fig. 26)**.

Fig. 26

Pull the thread almost all the way through, leaving a loose loop. Bring the needle through the loop **from front to back (Fig. 27)**.

Fig. 27

Continue in this way to finish your edge, securing with a knot.

Trimming Guide

Trimming a latch hook project is amazing. A pass over your finished work with a sharp pair of shears makes all the difference in the professionalism of a finished piece. Sins from the strand-making and knotting processes are cut away. Colorful images become exponentially more defined, allowing details to shine. Longer pile projects with the right fiber and density can be trimmed into three-dimensional shapes not unlike sculpting a piece of stone—only yarn is a lot easier to work with! Trimming is where the artistry comes in. As the maker, you get to make the call about whether and how much to trim, if you're going to stress about a uniform rug pile, how much curve you'd like your edge to have, and more.

I can't teach you how to cut a perfect dome in a craft book, but here are a few tips for trimming success that I swear by:

1. Don't over trim—you can always cut more yarn away, but you can't add it back once it's cut!

2. Do all of the finishing and binding called for in your pattern before trimming. Your rug pile will experience some shifting during the finishing and binding process, so leaving trimming for the end saves you from trimming more than once.

3. Once your finishing and binding are all set, give your work a gentle run through with your fingers. The goal here is to unearth surprise tangles and help yarn stand straight out from your canvas.

4. For those with perfection in mind, I also recommend the use of a not-too-strong hand vacuum after trimming. It's a really good way to clean up fuzz, but it also helps your project strands look their best after trimming.

5. If you're wanting to make multicolored projects more crisp-looking, separate large sections of color and trim them one color at a time before a final pass over the whole piece.

Backing & Hanging Guide

When your pattern calls for it, backing and hanging are the very last steps in the latch hook process. Backing and hanging present the most diversity in style and are dependent on what you're doing with your finished object. The following are common approaches to latch hook project backing:

- **Appliqué style:** If your project is hooked, finished and bound before mounting on a surface (like the Rainbow Back Patch, page 17), it doesn't need additional backing as the backing was provided by the surface on which it was mounted.
- **Flexible throw backing:** Very similar to appliqué-style backing, fabric is stitched onto the back of a project to cover all raw canvas (see Faux Shearling Throw, page 48).
- **Glue and felt:** See tutorial below.

  Large **Wall hangings** don't generally require backing (see Fried Egg Wall Hanging, page 57), though I prefer to back small wall hangings (see Sweet Lamb Wall Hanging, page 44) using the glue and felt method.
- **Simple Non-Skid Rug Backing:** See tutorial below.

Glue and Felt

Using a felt tip pen, trace and cut a piece of felt fabric big enough to cover the raw canvas backing of your project. Using a modest amount of Tacky Glue® and sewing clamps as needed, adhere the felt backing to your project and let dry completely **(Fig. 28)**.

Fig. 28

Simple Non-Skid Rug Backing

In general, I advocate the use of non-skid rug backing for latch hook rugs. You can get it very affordably at houseware stores, often coming in standard rug sizes (i.e. 8' x 10'). Grab a large size piece, and you can use it as you would fabric yardage, cutting from it as needed to back rug projects.

To back a latch hook rug in this way, begin by cutting an appropriately sized rectangle of non-skid rug backing, so a piece that is slightly smaller than your completed rug **(Fig. 29)**. The non-skid backing should be entirely hidden under the rug itself.

Fig. 29

You can center and Whipstitch the backing in place (**Fig. 30**), but if you're not a fan of hand sewing, you can use your rug backing as you would with a commercially-purchased rug: lay it on the ground and lay the rug on top. Done! The choice is yours.

Fig. 30

Basic Hanging Tips

When it comes to hanging a latch hook project on the wall for display, the approach can be simple. Pin a few safety pins to the back of an otherwise-completely finished project, through any backing and behind a couple squares of rug canvas to create a hook (**Fig. 31**). Catching the canvas is important because that's where the weight of your project lies. Once safety pins are attached, hang your project on a nail or wall hook. Straightforward hanging like this works for most smaller projects.

Fig. 31

For hanging a larger latch hook piece like the Fried Egg Wall Hanging (page 57), incorporate a wooden dowel at the back of your work to support the finished project. This is similar to shoring up a heavy section of strands, like the egg yolk from the aforementioned Wall Hanging, or attaching handles to the Fringed Party Bag (page 52). It's all the same concept: reinforce potentially weak areas to extend the life of your latch hook project. For hanging, the dowels function like the safety pins in the simpler approach, creating something that can be used for hanging with a hook/nail/string.

To incorporate a dowel for hanging, stitch a piece of canvas slightly larger than your dowel to the back of your project (just like patching in canvas as outlined on page 11). Working through both layers of canvas and using strong thread or yarn, Whipstitch your wooden dowel to the back of your work (**Fig. 32**).

Fig. 32

Rainbow Back Patch

Latch Hook Skill Level: **Beginner**
Hand Sewing Skill Level: **Experience Helpful**

Finished project size: **9" x 9"**

Pile Height = **1"**
Strand length = **2½"**
Strands per knot = **1**

INSTRUCTIONS

SUPPLIES LIST

- Patons® Classic Wool Worsted™ Yarn (100% wool; 100g /210 yds): 1 skein each Aran, Blue Fog, Bright Red, Honey, and New Denim
- Jean Jacket
- 3.75 mesh rug canvas
- Fabric marker
- Latch hook tool
- Sewing clamps or clothespins
- Sewing needle
- Sewing thread
- Scissors
- Tapestry (yarn) needle

SETUP

To prepare your project for hooking, cut a 13" x 13" square of 3.75 mesh rug canvas and a small amount of 2½" strands of each color of your project yarn. (If you run out, you can cut more.) Before you begin hooking, decide whether you will be using square or non-square finishing (see Finishing Guide, page 10) and prepare your canvas as needed.

1. Lay out your canvas piece, ensuring it is facing the correct direction (see Rug Canvas section, page 3).

2. Start your project centered on the canvas, leaving a minimum of 2" all around. Knot the design following the chart, page 20.

3. Once your project is hooked, hand finish your raw edges following the Finishing Guide, page 10, if you have not already done so. Then bind and trim your project following the Binding Guide, page 12, and the Trimming Guide, page 14.

4. Finally attach your patch to your jacket. Place the finished & bound patch on your jacket as desired. Clamp or pin your patch in place before Whipstitching (see Binding Guide page 12) around the canvas edge and into the fabric of your jacket to secure.

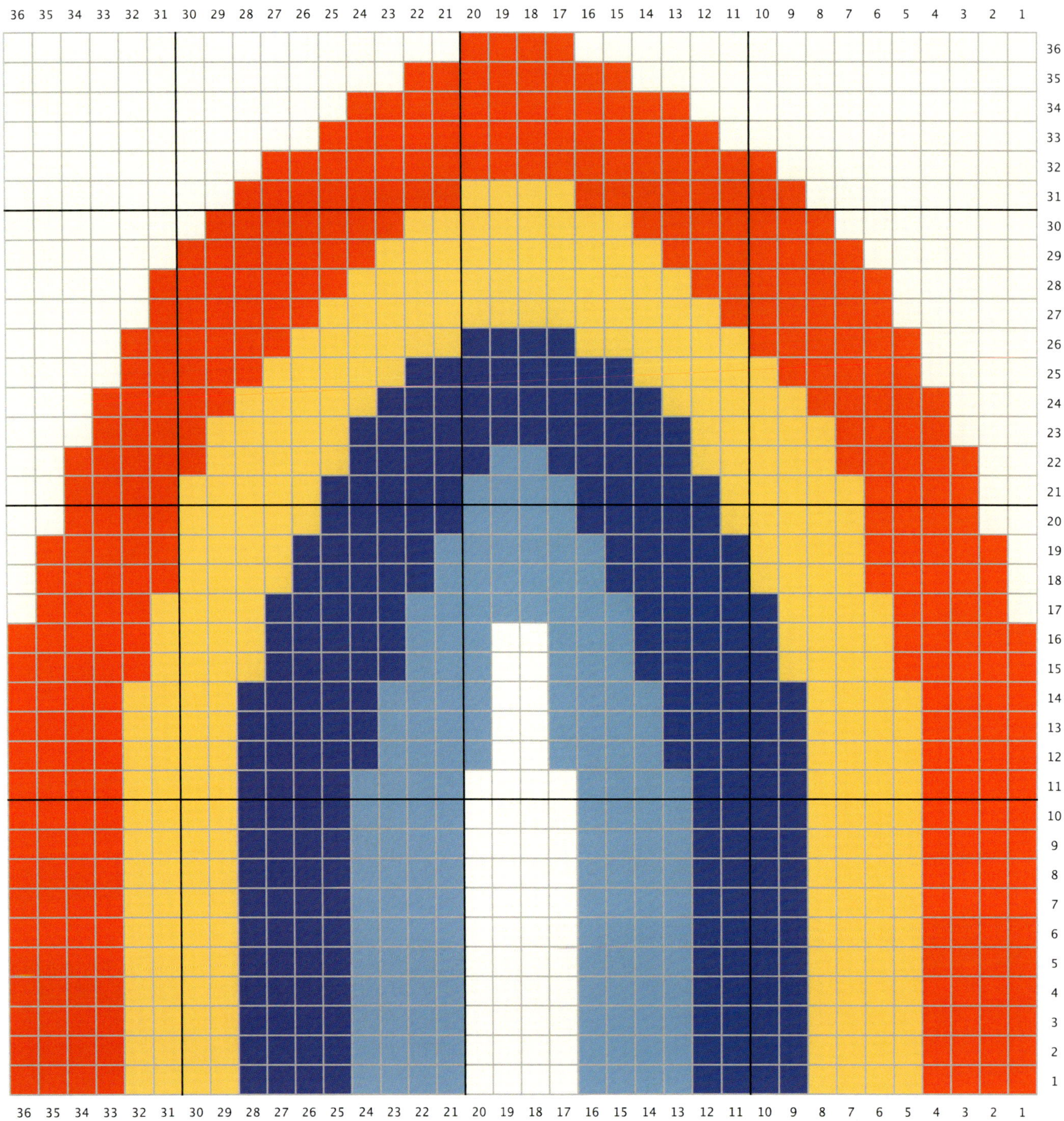

Color Key

One square = one knot

- Aran
- Honey
- Bright Red
- Blue Fog
- Blue Denim

Hey Welcome Mat

Latch Hook Skill Level: **Beginner**
Hand Sewing Skill Level: **Experience Helpful**

Finished project size: **14" x 25"**

Pile Height = **1½"**
Strand length = **3½"**
Strands per knot = **2**

INSTRUCTIONS

SUPPLIES LIST

- Lion Brand® Wool Ease® Yarn (80% acrylic/20% wool; 85g /197 yds): 6 skeins Blue Mist; 2 skeins Natural Heather
- 3.75 mesh rug canvas
- Latch hook tool
- Non-skid rug backing
- Sewing clamps or clothespins
- Sewing needle (optional)
- Sewing thread (optional)
- Scissors
- Tapestry (yarn) needle

SETUP

To prepare your project, cut an 18" tall x 29" wide piece of 3.75 mesh rug canvas with twisted strands running vertically. Leaving aside one full skein of Blue Mist yarn for finishing and binding, cut 3½" strands of each color of your project yarn. (If you run out, you can cut more.) Before you begin hooking, decide whether you will be using square or non-square finishing (see Finishing Guide, page 10) and prepare your canvas as needed.

1. Lay out your canvas piece, ensuring it is facing the correct direction (see Rug Canvas section, page 3).

2. Start your project centered on the canvas, leaving a minimum of 2" all around. Hold 2 strands of yarn together and knot the design following the chart, page 23.

3. Once your project is hooked, hand finish your raw edges following the Finishing Guide, page 10, if you have not already done so. Then bind and trim your project following the Binding Guide, page 12, and the Trimming Guide, page 14.

4. To back the mat, begin by cutting an appropriately-sized rectangle of non-skid rug backing (see Backing Guide, page 15). You can center and Whipstitch the backing in place or simply lay the backing on the ground and lay the rug on top.

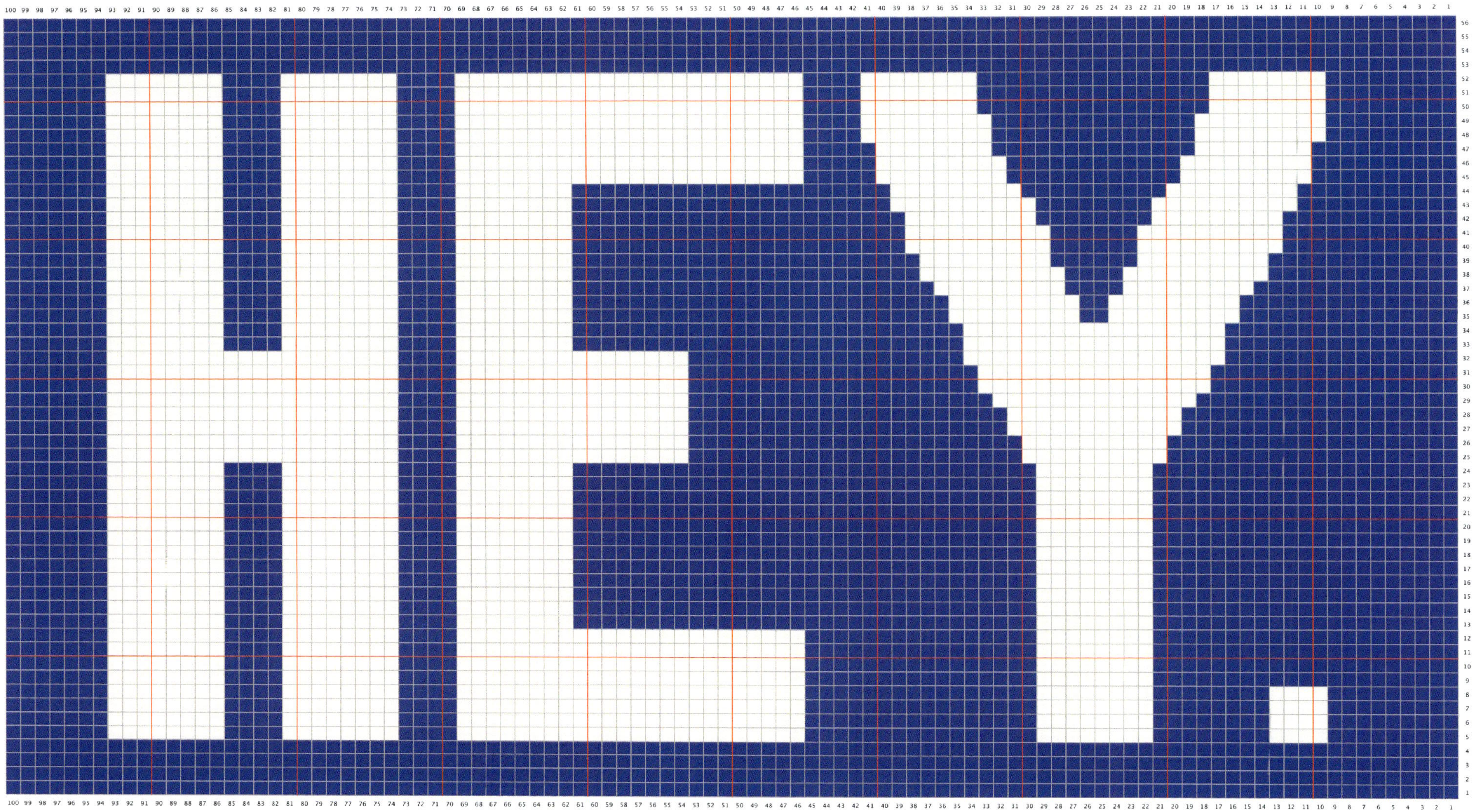

Color Key
One square = one knot

Blue Mist

Natural Heather

Sprinkle Stool Cover

Latch Hook Skill Level: **Beginner**
Hand Sewing Skill Level: **Experience Helpful**

Finished project size: **11" diameter circle**
(before attaching to stool)

Pile Height = **1"**
Strand length = **2½"**
Strands per knot = **1**

INSTRUCTIONS

SUPPLIES LIST

- Patons® Classic Wool Worsted™ Yarn (100% wool; 100g/210 yds): 1 skein each Aran, Blue Fog, Bright Red, Honey, and New Denim
- 3.75 mesh rug canvas
- Latch hook tool
- Sewing clamps or clothespins
- Sewing needle
- Sewing thread
- Scissors
- Staple gun (optional)
- 11" diameter stool with optional removable cover
- Tapestry (yarn) needle

SETUP

To prepare your project, cut a 15" x 15" piece of 3.75 mesh rug canvas and a small amount of 2½" strands of each color of your project yarn. (Cut more 2½" strands as necessary.) Be sure to leave 10 yards of at least one of the colors for finishing and binding.

1. Lay out your canvas piece, ensuring it is facing the correct direction (see Rug Canvas section, page 3).

2. Start your project centered on the canvas, leaving a minimum of 2" all around. Knot the design following the chart, page 27. (If your stool is a different size, you may still work from the chart, but it will be up to you to determine how to alter its size.)

3. Once your project is hooked, hand finish your raw edges following the Finishing Guide, page 10, if you have not already done so. Then bind and trim your project following Binding Guide, page 12, and Trimming Guide, page 14.

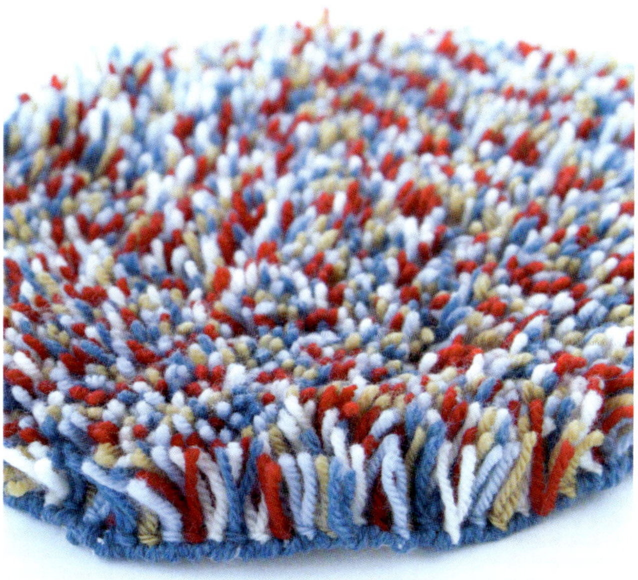

4. Whipstitch (see Binding Guide, page 12) the circle-shaped latch hook piece to the top of the cover that came with the stool. And if your stool doesn't have a cover, there are a few options. If you can sew, sew a fabric cover similar to the one pictured. You may alternately staple gun your latch hook piece directly to the stool through your rug canvas.

5. No matter your stool attachment method, the final step is to take an eye-level look at your stool with the cover in place. If you've got a strand or two out of place, this is the time to spot-trim for a professional finish.

Color Key
One square = one knot

- Bright Red
- Blue Fog
- New Denim
- Aran
- Honey
- No knot

Faux Fur Peter Pan Collar

Latch Hook Skill Level:
Confident Beginner
Hand Sewing Skill Level:
Experienced

Finished project size:
Each half measures approximately 5" x 2¾"

Pile Height = **1½"**
Strand length = **3½"**
Strands per knot = **1**

INSTRUCTIONS

SUPPLIES LIST

- Patons® Classic Wool Roving® (100% wool; 100g/120yds): 1 skein each Aran, Cherry, Royal, and Yellow
- 3.75 mesh rug canvas
- Felt for backing
- Felt tip pen
- Latch hook tool
- Ribbon: two 8" -10" lengths (your choice of color)
- Scissors
- Sewing needle
- Sewing clamps or clothespins
- Strong sewing thread
- Tacky Glue®
- Tapestry (yarn) needle

SETUP

To prepare your project, cut two pieces of 3.75 mesh canvas that measure 9" wide x 6¾" tall with twisted strands running vertically. Cut a small amount of 3½" strands of each color of your project yarn (cut more as needed). Be sure to leave a few yards of yarn for finishing and binding.

1. Lay out your canvas piece, ensuring it is facing the correct direction (see Rug Canvas section, page 3).

2. Starting with each half of your project centered on its piece of canvas to accommodate 2" seam allowance, knot each half of the collar design following the charts, page 30. Once both are hooked, hand finish your raw canvas (Finishing Guide, page 10).

3. Bind each half of the collar's edges (see Binding Guide, page 12). Please note that even though it's a small project, this Collar requires a fair bit of hand sewing to finish due to its unique shape and small size.

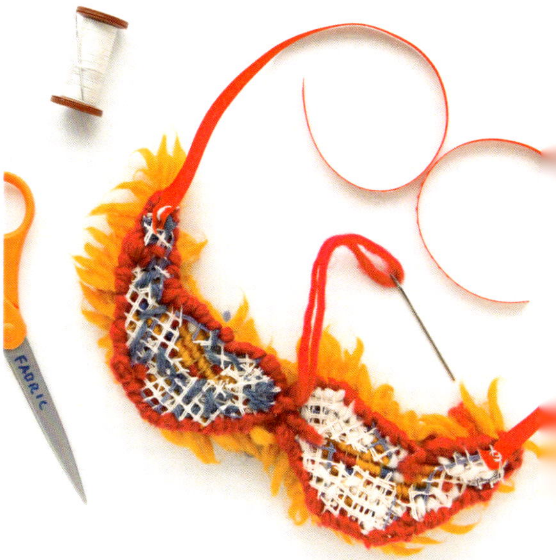

4. Using Whipstitch (page 12), sew the halves of the collar together at the center.

5. Sew an 8" -10" length of ribbon to each corner of the collar. Use strong sewing thread as the weight of the collar will rest on these stitches.

6. Trace and cut a piece of felt to cover the raw canvas backing of your collar. Using a modest amount of Tacky Glue® and sewing clamps, adhere the felt backing to the collar and let dry completely.

7. Finally trim your collar however you like (see Trimming Guide, page 14). The pictured sample was fairly aggressively trimmed to take advantage of the roving style yarn!

Color Key
One square = one knot

- Royal
- Yellow
- No knot
- Cherry
- Aran

LEFT

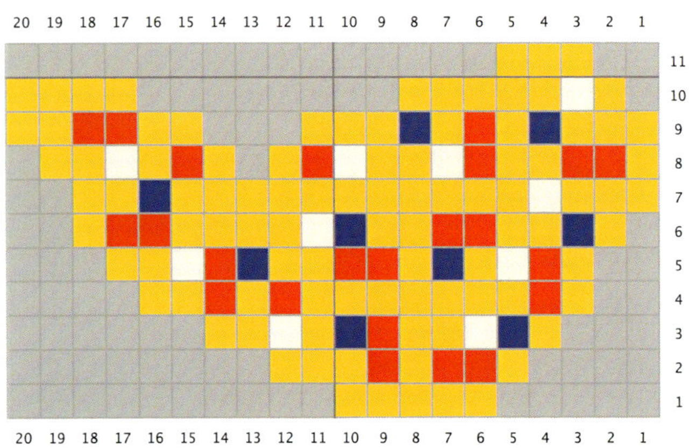

RIGHT

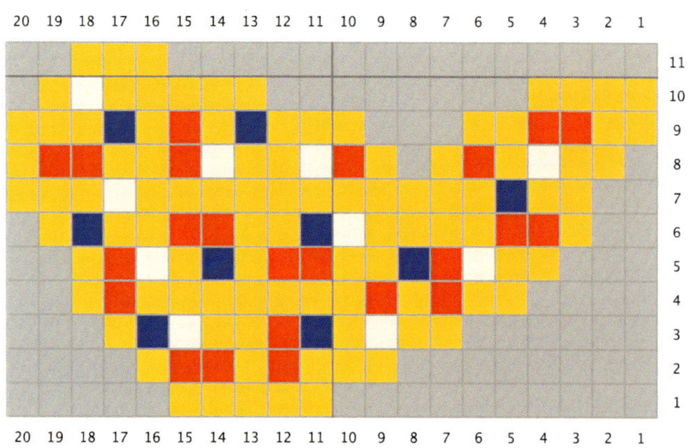

Layered Heart Tote

Latch Hook Skill Level: **Confident Beginner**
Hand Sewing Skill Level: **Experienced**

Finished project size: **13" x 13" (**before attaching to bag)

Pile Height ranges from **2¾" to 3¾"**
Strand Lengths range from **6" to 8"**
Strands per knot = **1**

SUPPLIES LIST

- Lion Brand® Wool Ease® Yarn (80% acrylic/20% wool; 85g /197 yds): 1 skein each Cranberry, Natural Heather, and Rose Heather
- 3.75 mesh rug canvas
- Latch hook tool
- Sewing clamps or clothespins
- Sewing needle
- Sewing thread
- Scissors
- Tapestry (yarn) needle
- Tote bag measuring at least 14" x 14"

SETUP

To prepare your project, cut a piece of 3.75 mesh canvas that measures 17½" x 17½". Leaving several yards of Cranberry yarn for finishing and binding, cut 8" strands of Cranberry yarn, 7" strands of Rose Heather, and 6" of Natural Heather. For the Layered Heart Tote, varying strand lengths are used to give some 3-dimensionality to the project, so you don't have to rely exclusively on trimming to shape.

INSTRUCTIONS

1. Lay out your canvas piece, ensuring it is facing the correct direction (see Rug Canvas section, page 3).

2. Start your project centered on the canvas, leaving a minimum of 2" all around. Knot the design following the chart, page 34.

3. Once your project is hooked, hand finish your raw edges following the Finishing Guide, page 10, if you have not already done so. As mentioned in the Finishing Guide, patching in scrap canvas can be helpful for reinforcing heavier latch hook projects.

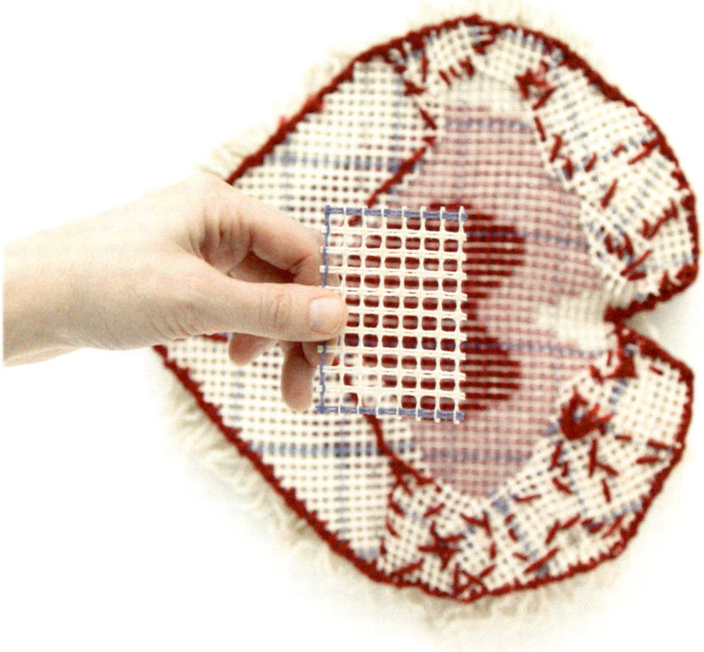

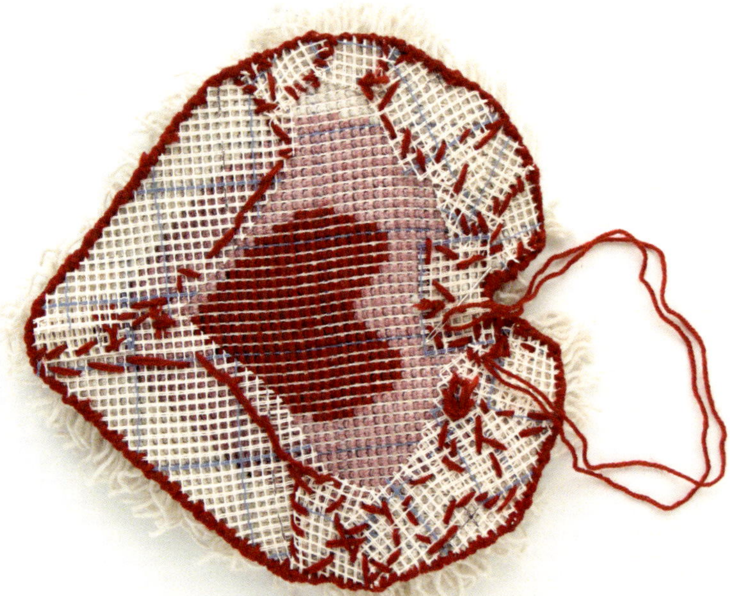

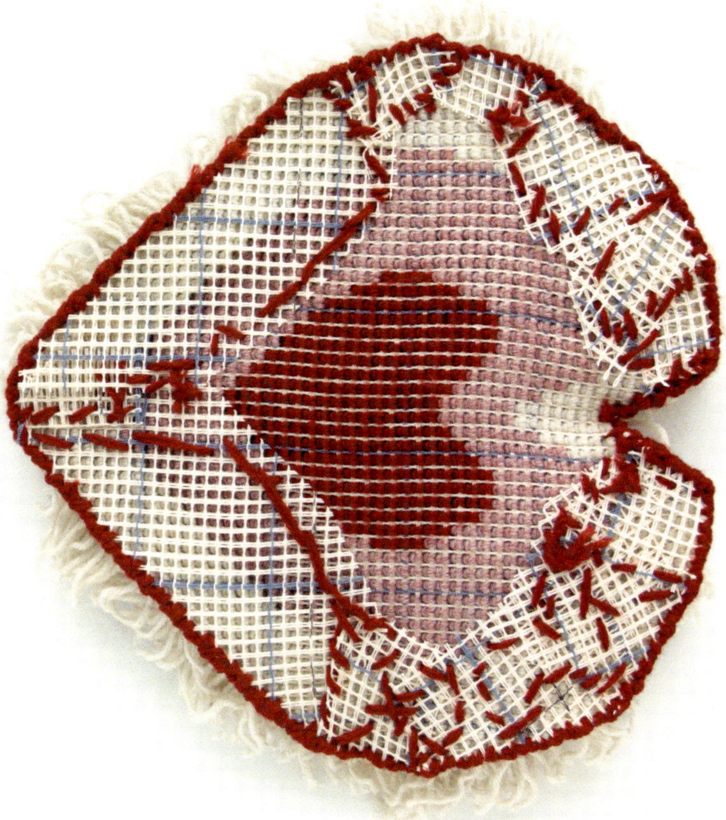

4. Bind the heart's edges (see Binding Guide, page 12) before trimming (see Trimming Guide, page 14).

5. Center the heart on your tote bag and use sewing clamps to hold in place. Whipstitch (see Binding Guide, page 12) all the way around, catching the canvas of your tote and heart latch hook under the needle to appliqué it to the tote.

Color Key
One square = one knot

- Natural Heather
- Rose Heather
- Cranberry
- No knot

Chompy, A Hinged Wall Hanging

Latch Hook Skill Level: **Confident Beginner**
Hand Sewing Skill Level: **Experienced**

Finished project size: **Upper Panel 9" x 8"; Lower Panel 9" x 4"**

Pile Height = **1½"**
Strand lengths = **3½"**
Strands per knot = **2**

SUPPLIES LIST

- **Lion Brand® Wool Ease® Yarn (80% acrylic/20% wool; 85g /197 yds): 1 skein each Blue Mist, Fisherman, and Ranch Red**
- **3.75 mesh rug canvas**
- **Felt for backing**
- **Felt tip pen**
- **Latch hook tool**
- **Scissors**
- **Sewing clamps or clothespins**
- **Tacky Glue®**
- **Tapestry (yarn) needle**

SETUP

To prepare your project, cut two pieces of 3.75 mesh canvas with twisted strands running vertically: one that measures 13" wide x 12" tall and one that measures 13" wide x 8" tall. Cut 3½" strands of each color of your project yarn (cut more as needed). Be sure to leave a few yards of yarn for finishing and binding.

INSTRUCTIONS

1. Lay out your canvas piece, ensuring it is facing the correct direction (see Rug Canvas section, page 3).

2. Start your project centered on the canvas, leaving a minimum of 2" all around. Hold 2 strands of yarn together and knot the design following the charts, page 38.

3. Once your project is hooked, hand finish any remaining raw edges. For an irregularly-shaped project like Chompy, you will need to trim and patch in reinforcement canvas as you work to finish all the edges of the "teeth" in particular. Just be careful during this step to not over trim your canvas as it will result in weak edges that may be susceptible to fraying. For instruction on all of this, see Finishing Guide, page 10.

4. Next, securely bind all edges (see Binding Guide, page 12). With Chompy's angular teeth, carefully binding its edges is an important step to ensure the structural soundness of the finished project.

5. Back each panel with felt and glue following the Backing and Hanging Guide, page 15. Let dry entirely before Whipstitching (page 12) the upper and lower sections together.

6. Trim project to an all over, even pile (see Trimming Guide, page 14).

7. To hang, employ the safety pin method (see Backing and Hanging Guide, page 15).

UPPER

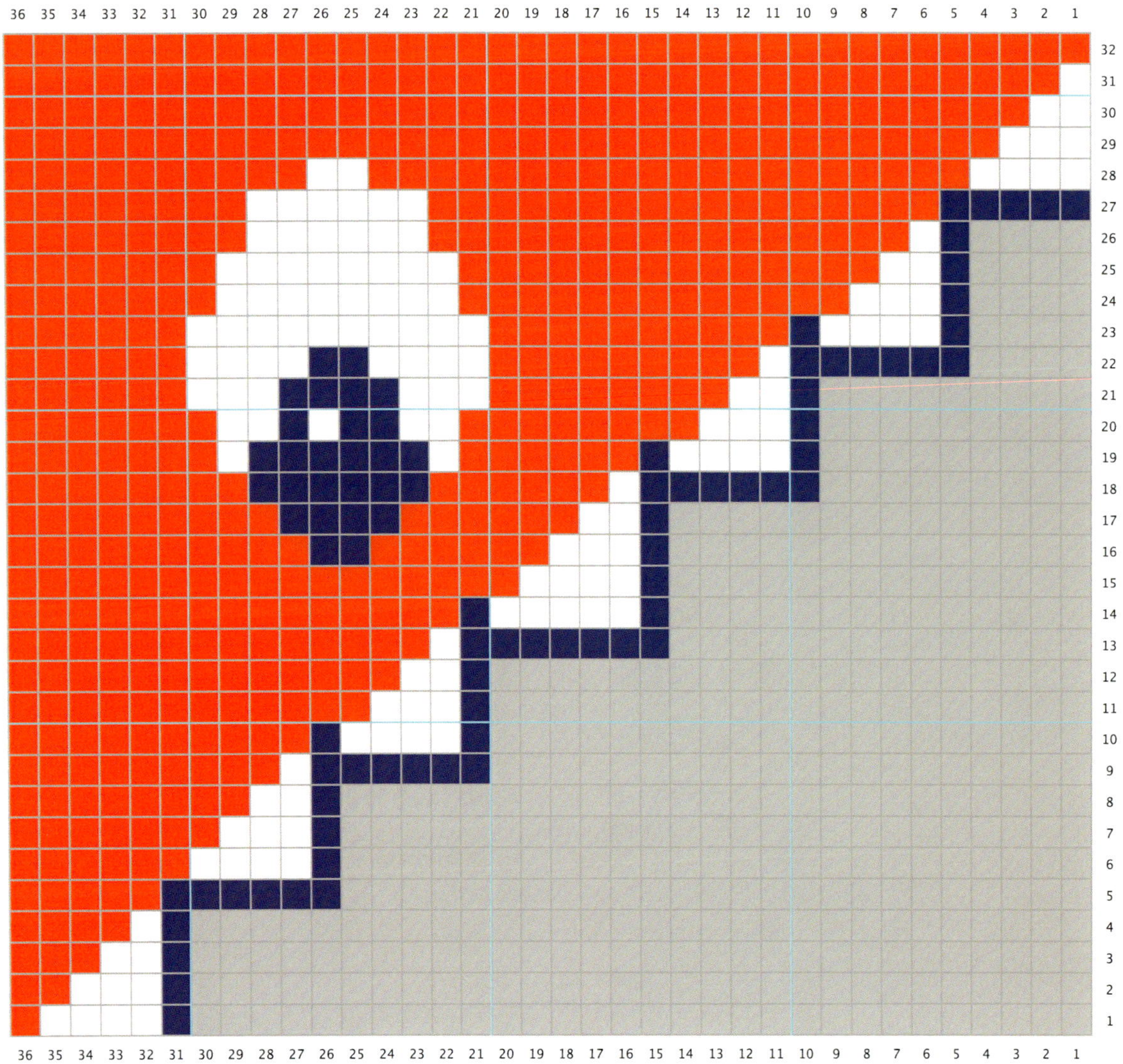

Color Key
One square = one knot

- Fisherman
- Ranch Red
- Blue Mist
- No knot

LOWER

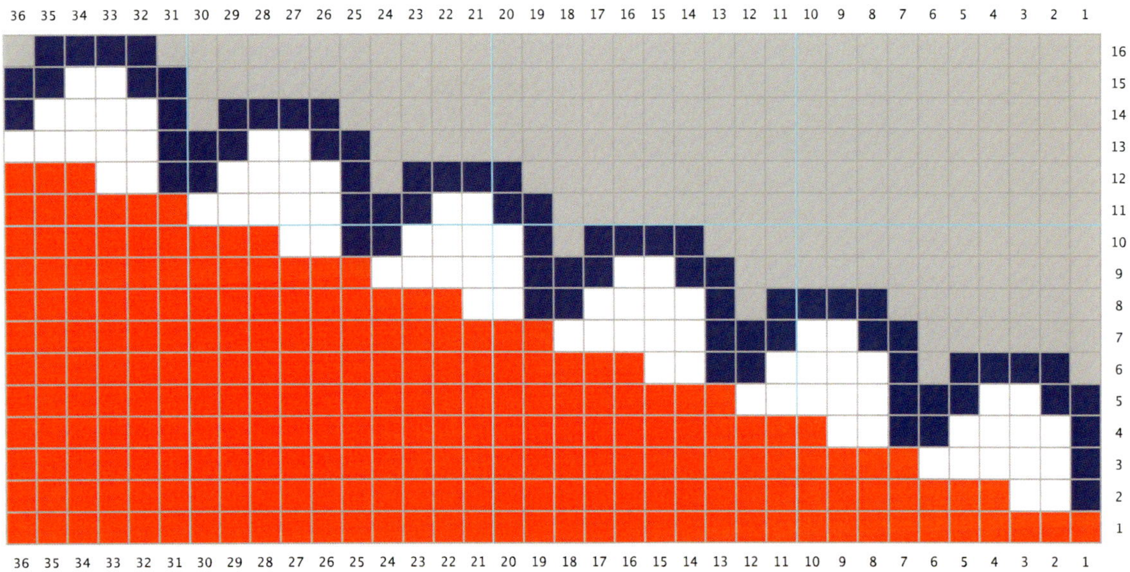

Blue Jay and Cardinal Wall Hangings

The Blue Jay & Cardinal Wall Hangings are two separate projects, designed to complement each other. Over the next few pages, I'll walk you through how to complete either of them—the instructions are the same for both.

Latch Hook Skill Level: **Confident Beginner**
Hand Sewing Skill Level: **Experienced**

Finished project size: **13" x 10"**

Pile Height = **1¼"**
Strand lengths = **3"**
Strands per knot = **2**

SUPPLIES LIST

- LB Collection® Superwash Merino Yarn (100% Superwash Merino Wool; 100g/306yds)
  - Colors for Blue Jay: 1 skein each Antique, Denim, Midnight Blue, Moonstone, and Night Sky
  - Colors for Cardinal: 1 skein each Antique, Cayenne, Cherry, Mustard Seed, Moonstone, Night Sky, and Persimmon
- 5 mesh rug canvas
- Felt for backing
- Felt tip pen
- Latch hook tool
- Scissors
- Sewing clamps or clothespins
- Tacky Glue®
- Tapestry (yarn) needle

SETUP

To make either bird, cut a single piece of 5 mesh canvas that measures 17" wide x 14" tall with twisted strands running vertically. Cut 3" strands of each color of your project yarn. Be sure to leave several yards of yarn for finishing and binding.

INSTRUCTIONS

1. Lay out your canvas piece, ensuring it is facing the correct direction (see Rug Canvas section, page 3).

2. Start your project centered on the canvas, leaving a minimum of 2" all around. Hold 2 strands of yarn together and knot the design following the chart, pages 42 or 43).

3. Hand finish your canvas edges (see Finishing Guide, page 10). Remember, for an irregularly-shaped project like a bird with a thin tail, patching in canvas and overlapping seam allowances are great ways to reinforce your project at weak points!

4. Next, bind all edges (see Binding Guide, page 12).

5. Back each panel with felt and glue following the Backing and Hanging Guide, page 15.

6. Trim project to an all over, even pile (see Trimming Guide, page 14).

7. To hang, employ the safety pin method (see Backing and Hanging Guide, page 15).

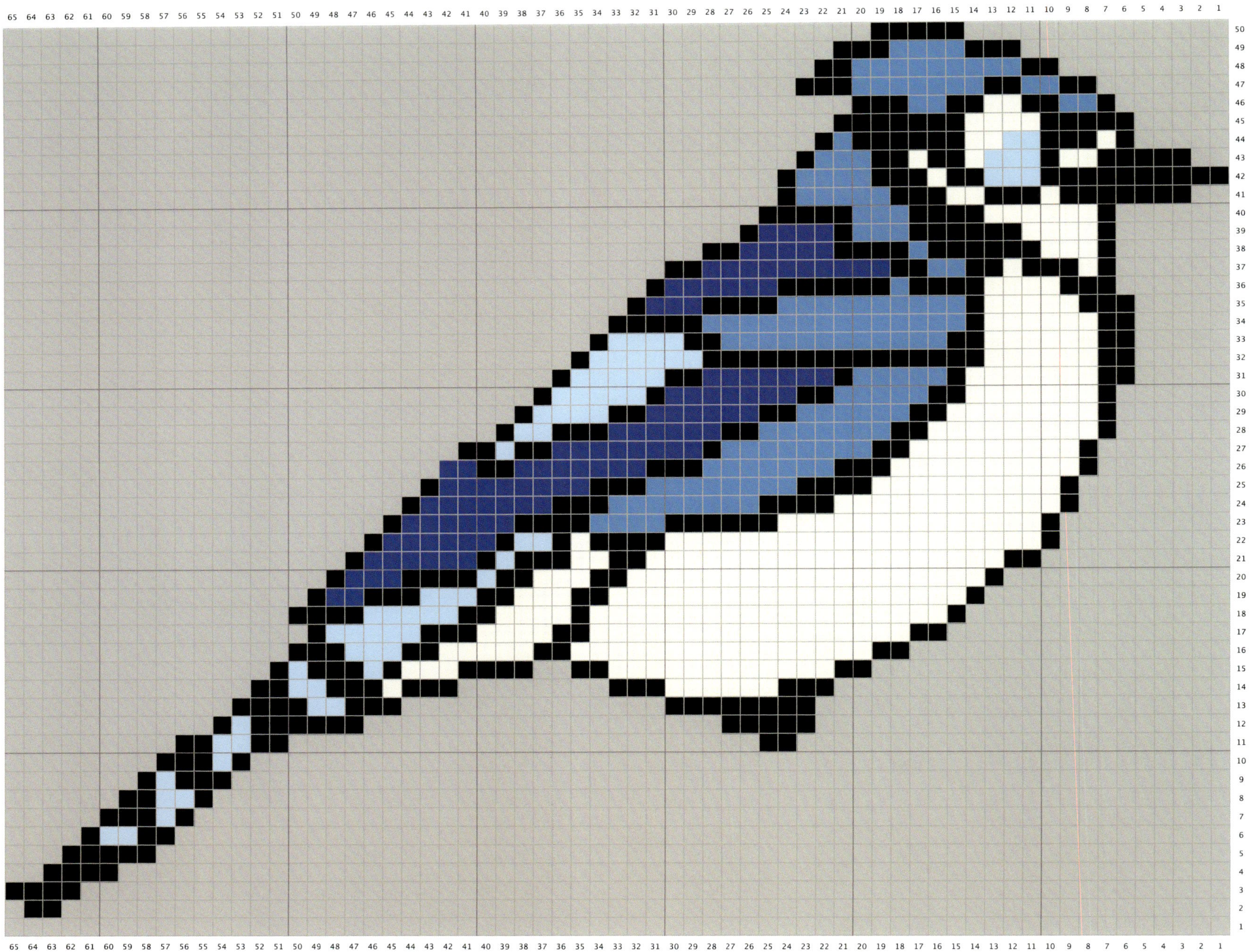

Color Key
One square = one knot

- Night Sky
- No knot
- Midnight Blue
- Denim
- Moonstone
- Antique

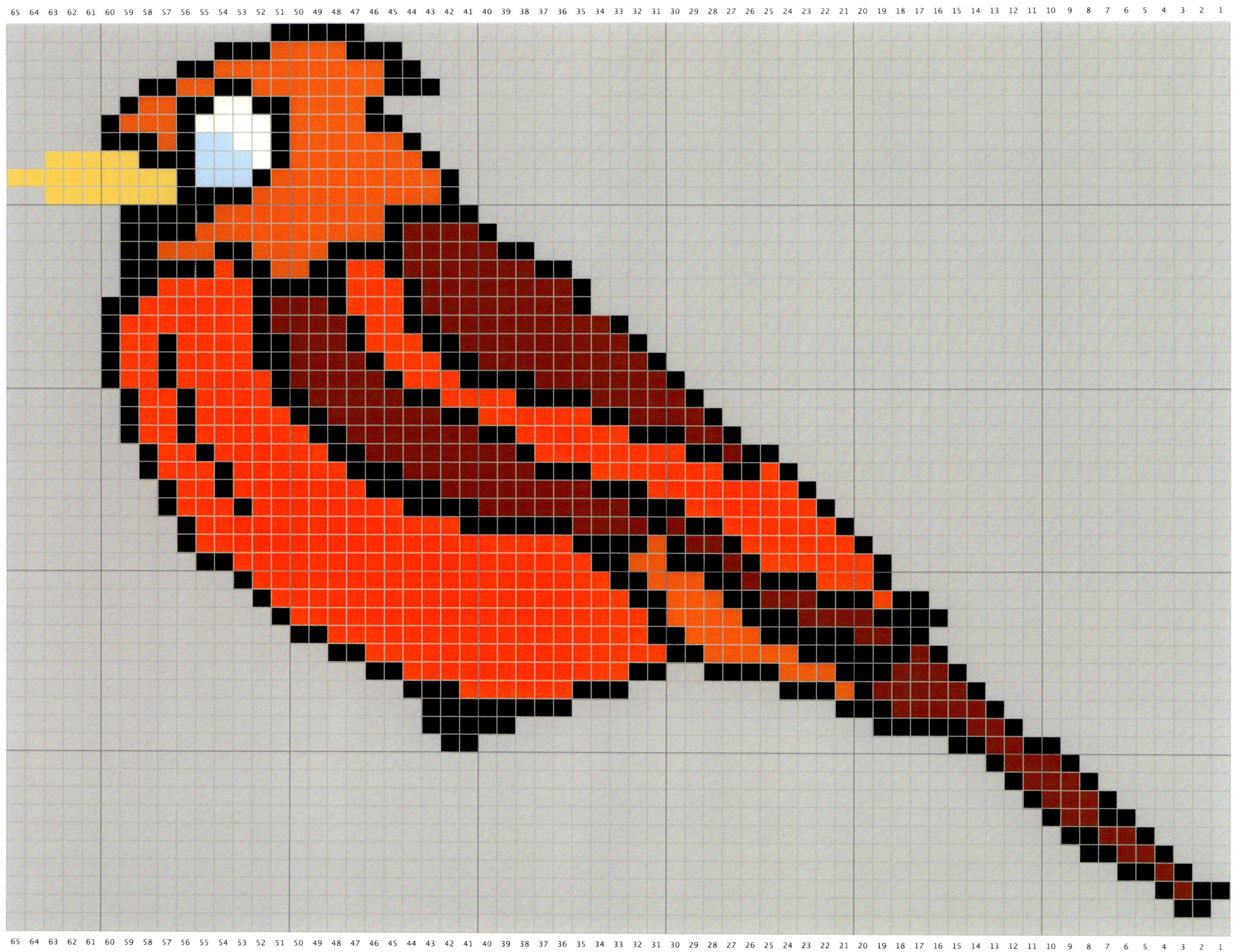

Color Key
One square = one knot

- Mustard Seed
- No knot
- Cherry
- Persimmon
- Night Sky
- Antique
- Cayenne
- Moonstone

Sweet Lamb Wall Hanging

Latch Hook Skill Level: **Confident Beginner**
Hand Sewing Skill Level: **Experienced**

Finished project size: **12" x 12"**

Pile Height = **1¼"**
Strand length = **3"**
Strands per knot = **2**

INSTRUCTIONS

SUPPLIES LIST

- LB Collection® Superwash Merino Yarn (100% Superwash Merino Wool; 100g/306yds) 1 skein each Antique, Denim, Midnight Blue, Moonstone, and Mustard Seed
- 5 mesh rug canvas
- Felt for backing
- Felt tip pen
- Latch hook tool
- Scissors
- Sewing clamps or clothespins
- Tacky Glue®
- Tapestry (yarn) needle

SETUP

Cut a piece of 5 mesh canvas that measures 16" x 16" . Cut 3" strands of each color of your project yarn. Be sure to leave several yards of yarn for finishing and binding.

1. Lay out your canvas piece, ensuring it is facing the correct direction (see Rug Canvas section, page 3).

2. Start your project centered on the canvas, leaving a minimum of 2" all around. Hold 2 strands of yarn together and knot the design following the charts, page 47.

3. Hand finish your raw canvas (see Finishing Guide, page 10). The Sweet Lamb Wall Hanging has a complex silhouette, making it a great candidate for patching in extra scraps of canvas for reinforcement in funny little nooks and crannies.

4. Next, bind all edges (see Binding Guide, page 12)

5. Back each panel with felt and glue following the Backing and Hanging Guide, page 15.

6. Trim project to an all over, even pile (see Trimming Guide, page 14).

7. To hang, employ the safety pin method (see Backing and Hanging Guide, page 15).

Color Key

One square = one knot

- Denim
- Midnight Blue
- Mustard Seed
- Moonstone
- Antique
- No knot

Faux Shearling Throw

Latch Hook Skill Level: **Intermediate**
Hand Sewing Skill Level: **Confident**

Finished project size: **24" x 36"**

Pile Height = **2¼"**
Strand length = **5"**
Strands per knot = **1**

SUPPLIES LIST

- Lion Brand® Touch of Mohair Yarn (90% acrylic, 10% mohair; 100g/339yds): 9 skeins Gardenia
- 5 mesh rug canvas
- Felt or other fabric for backing, at least 24" x 36"
- Felt tip pen or chalk (for tracing fabric backing)
- Latch hook tool
- Permanent marker
- Scissors
- Sewing clamps or clothespins
- Tapestry (yarn) needle

SETUP

Cut a piece of 5 mesh canvas that measures 28" wide x 40" tall with twisted strands running vertically. Cut 5" strands of your project yarn, leaving 2 full skeins for finishing and binding.

INSTRUCTIONS

1. Draw your Throw. The Faux Shearling Throw is not worked from a chart. Instead, begin by freehand drawing the silhouette of a sheepskin on your 28" x 40" canvas using a permanent marker. (Don't worry, I can't draw either and managed well enough. Your throw can also be an abstract shape—this is YOUR project!) Don't forget to leave at least 2" of seam allowance on all sides for finishing. Let ink dry completely.

2. Hook your Throw. Lay out your canvas piece, ensuring it is facing the correct direction (see Rug Canvas section, page 3).

3. Working within your hand-drawn outline, hook your faux sheepskin by using one strand to knot every open square within your design on the canvas.

4. Hand finish your project edges following the Finishing Guide, page 10.

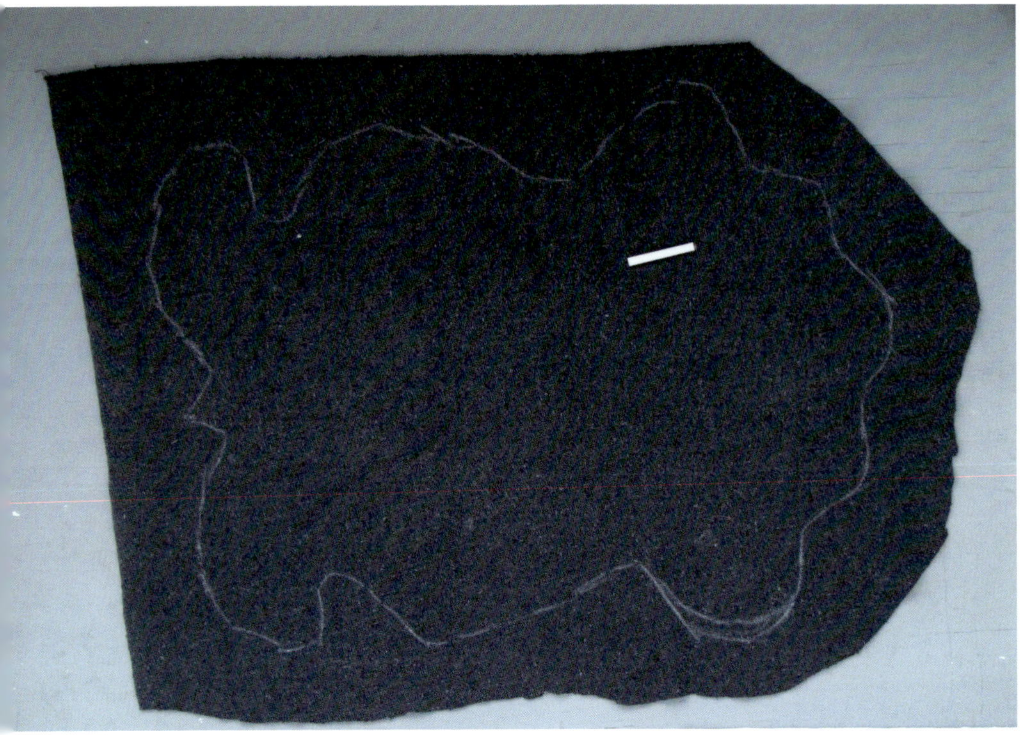

5. Create a fabric backing. The Faux Shearling Throw is backed and bound in one fell swoop, which is accomplished as you cover all of the raw canvas at the back of the Throw with a fabric backing. Begin by tracing the outline of your finished rug canvas onto a piece of fabric that measures at least 24" x 36" . Cut out your fabric backing. It should be exactly the same size as the finished canvas back of your hooked & finished Throw *without* any seam allowance.

6. Tie your throw. If you're familiar with quilting, there's a step called tying that you're going to employ next to complete your Throw. Align your fabric backing perfectly with the raw canvas side of your work. Use sewing clamps to hold backing in place. Thread your tapestry (yarn) needle with several inches of project yarn doubled up. Beginning at the front (fuzzy side) of your work, sew the yarn through your canvas and fabric backing. Leave at least 5" of yarn at the front of your work. Sew the yarn back through the fabric backing and canvas to the front.

7. Align your yarn tails at the front of your work, and hand knot them around an intersection of canvas strands. You may use as many ties as you wish, though evenly placing about 6 or 8 ties across your Throw should do the trick.

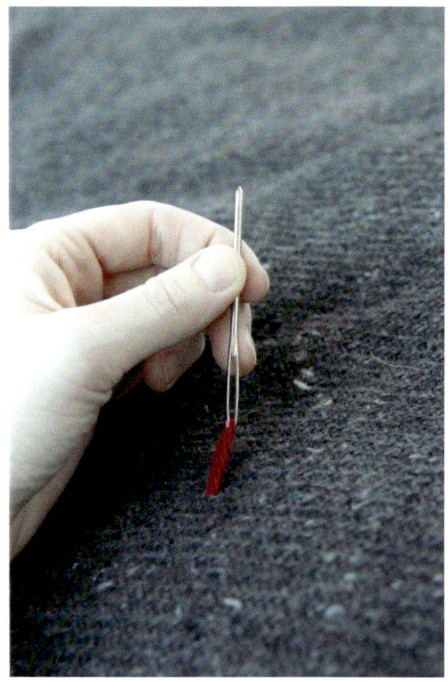

8. Back your Throw. Working all the way around the perimeter of your work, sew your fabric to the back of your work using Blanket Stitch (NOT Whipstitch as many other projects in this book call for—see Blanket Stitch, page 13). Use Blanket Stitch to finish the fabric backing's raw edge as well as attach the backing to the project. Since this is a throw, the backing has to be hand sewn to the latch hook piece to achieve a flexible blanket as well as effectively finishing the edge of the fabric backing. Trim excess backing fabric as needed.

9. Trim project to an all over, even pile (see Trimming Guide, page 14).

Fringed Party Bag

Latch Hook Skill Level: **Intermediate**
Hand Sewing Skill Level: **Confident**

Finished project size: **10" wide x 5" tall** (not including handles)

Pile Length = **6¾"**
Strand length = **14"**
Strands per knot = **2**

INSTRUCTIONS

SUPPLIES LIST

- Aunt Lydia's® Metallic™ Crochet Thread Size 10 (88% cotton, 12% metallic; 100yds): 21 skeins in Natural/Gold
- 5 mesh rug canvas
- Felt for lining, cut to 9½" x 9½"
- Latch hook tool
- Permanent marker
- Purse handles
- Scissors
- Sewing clamps or clothespins
- Sewing needle
- Sewing thread
- Tapestry (yarn) needle

SETUP

To prepare your project, cut two pieces of 5 mesh canvas that measure 14" wide x 10½" tall with twisted strands running vertically. Cut 14" strands of your project thread leaving one extra skein for finishing and binding. Before you begin hooking, decide whether you will be incorporating square or non-square finishing on right and left edges only (see Finishing Guide, page 10) and prepare your canvas as needed.

1. Draw your panel. The Fringed Party Bag is not worked from a chart. Instead, begin by drawing a 10" wide x 5" tall rectangle, centered on each piece of your 14" wide x 10½" tall canvas, using a permanent marker. Leave 2¾" (that extra seam allowance is important!) of seam allowance at the top and bottom and 2" of seam allowance on each side for finishing. Let ink dry completely.

2. Lay out your canvas piece, ensuring it is facing the correct direction (see Rug Canvas section. page 3).

3. Hook your panel. Working within your hand-drawn outline, hook your bag by using two strands to knot every open square within your design on the canvas.

4. Finish the sides. If you haven't already done so, finish the right and left edges of your canvas (see Finishing Guide, page 10), trimming the excess square notch of fabric at each corner.

5. Finish the top & bottom to reinforce. Like all latch hook projects with a long pile, the Fringed Party Bag has some weight to it. Since your rug canvas forms the structure of your finished bag, finishing and binding are where the work happens to ensure the strength of your finished project. To finish the top & bottom and reinforce your panel, fold the top and bottom seam allowance canvas toward each other so a couple of squares of mesh overlap at the back of your work. Carefully trim any unnecessary canvas.

6. Gather your sewing clamps, a tapestry needle, scissors and project thread. Using Whipstitch or Blanket Stitch (see Binding Guide, page 12), sew the overlapping squares of canvas together and to the back of your work. This process joins three sturdy layers of canvas, adding structure to the Bag.

7. Repeat Steps 2-6 to make the second purse panel.

8. Bind your panel. Finally, bind all edges with Whipstitch (see Binding Guide, page 12).

9. Join panels at the base. When both panels are finished and bound, stitch them together at the base using Blanket Stitch. (Blanket Stitch is recommended here because it provides better coverage than Whipstitch.) As you stitch, use the grid of the canvas as a guide to keep your panels aligned.

10. Attach purse handles. Attach the purse's handles per package directions using extra canvas reinforced with Blanket Stitch as shown.

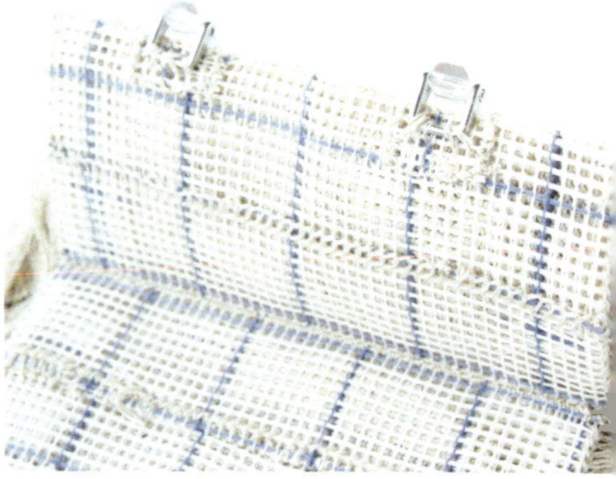

Top and bottom edge joining detail, plus binding.

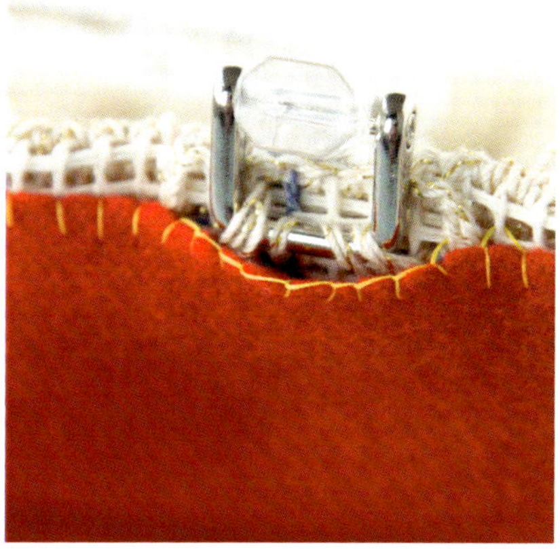

11. Line purse. Blanket Stitch a 9½" x 9½" square of felt onto the canvas interior of the bag, creatively avoiding the handles if necessary.

I used colorful felt and sewing thread to give my bag some added intrigue, but you can go as demure as you prefer.

12. Join panels at the sides. Finally, seam the bag's sides together with Blanket Stitch, aligning the grid of the canvas for symmetry and even stitches.

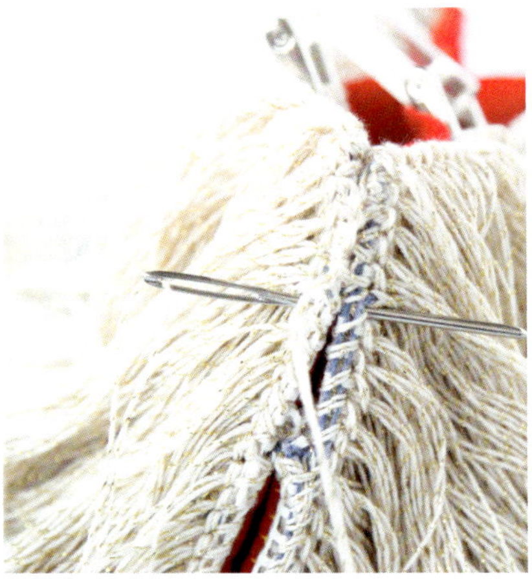

13. Trim as needed (see Trimming Guide, page 14), and you're ready to party!

Fried Egg Wall Hanging

Latch Hook Skill Level: **Intermediate**
Hand Sewing Skill Level: **Confident**

Finished project size: **37½" x 25"**

Pile Height ranges from **1" to 3½"**
Strand lengths range from **2½" to 7½"**
Strands per knot = **1**

SUPPLIES LIST

- Patons® Classic Wool Roving® (100% wool; 100g/120yds): 4 skeins Aran, 3 skeins Royal, and 3 skeins Yellow
- Worsted weight yarn (for finishing) in any similar color
- 3.75 mesh rug canvas
- Two 48" dowels (for hanging)
- Felt
- Felt tip marker
- Latch hook tool
- Scissors
- Sewing clamps or clothespins
- Tapestry (yarn) needle

SETUP

Cut a piece of 3.75 mesh canvas that measures 41½" wide x 29" tall with twisted strands running vertically. Cut 3 skeins of Yellow yarn into 7½" strands for the yolk, as well as exactly forty 7½" strands of Aran yarn for the "glare" of the egg yolk. Then cut the remaining Aran yarn and 3 additional skeins into 2½" strands. Also cut two full skeins of Royal into 2½" strands. Leave 1 skein of Royal for binding. Worsted weight yarn will be used for finishing.

INSTRUCTIONS

1. Lay out your canvas piece, ensuring it is facing the correct direction (see Rug Canvas section, page 3).

2. Start your project centered on the canvas, leaving a minimum of 2" all around. Knot the design following the charts, pages 60–63.

3. For the "egg white" you'll use 2½" strands of Aran and Royal yarn, and for the yolk, you'll use 7½" strands of Aran and Yellow.

This large project is worked over a single piece of canvas, so even though the charts are broken into 4 pieces to accommodate the physical size of a book page, you work from them as one to hook your egg.

4. Hand finish your raw canvas using *worsted weight yarn* (see Finishing Guide, page 10). Just like other projects in this book, the Egg requires hand sewn, non-square finishing and patching in extra canvas as you see fit to reinforce potentially precarious curves. The more canvas patching the better, including behind and around the egg yolk, to accommodate the weight of the long pile in that section of the project and the larger scale of the project overall.

5. Bind all edges using Patons® Classic Wool Roving™ in Royal (see Binding Guide, page 12).

6. Trim the "egg white" as needed to even out your work (see Trimming Guide, page 14). To achieve a sculpted, dome-like "yolk," this project will need to be tufted, though it can be left as-is if you're not confident in trimming. If you start slow and keep the image of an over easy egg in your head, the trimming is actually pretty easy. The roving style yarn is very forgiving. As always, start with a modest trim and continue as your confidence builds. As you work, outlying fibers will start to become more and more obvious, and in the end, you'll make the call about when you're happy with the finished look.

7. Whipstitch (page 12) a couple of appropriately-sized dowels to the back of your Egg, incorporating another strip of canvas in between for reinforcement (see Backing and Hanging Guide, page 15). The dowels add structure to the egg, in addition to giving you something to hang the egg from. Putting stress on the dowel instead of the canvas itself is a good idea for long-term hanging of a heavier item like this.

UPPER LEFT

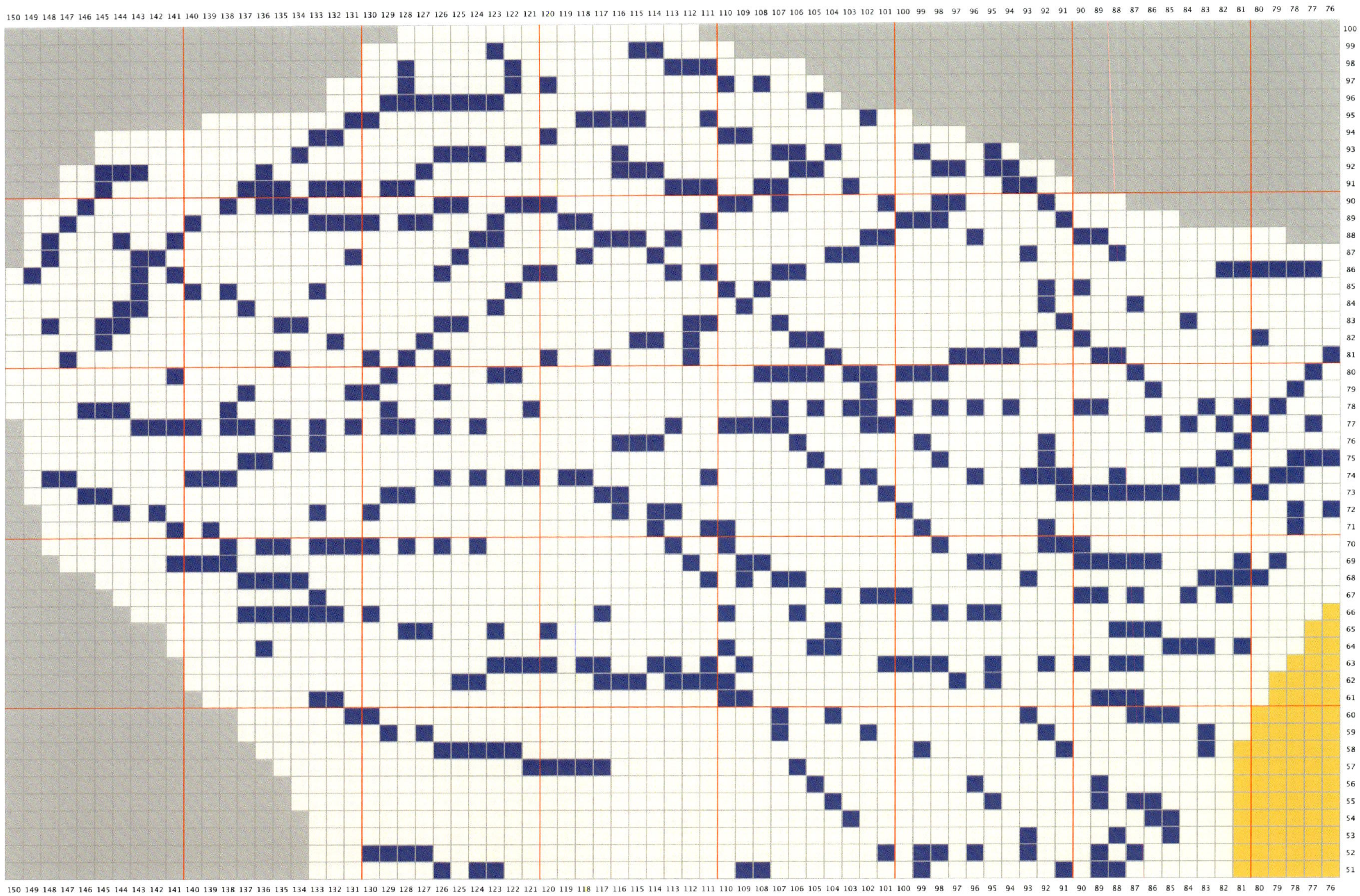

Color Key
One square = one knot

- Royal
- Aran
- Yellow
- No knot

UPPER RIGHT

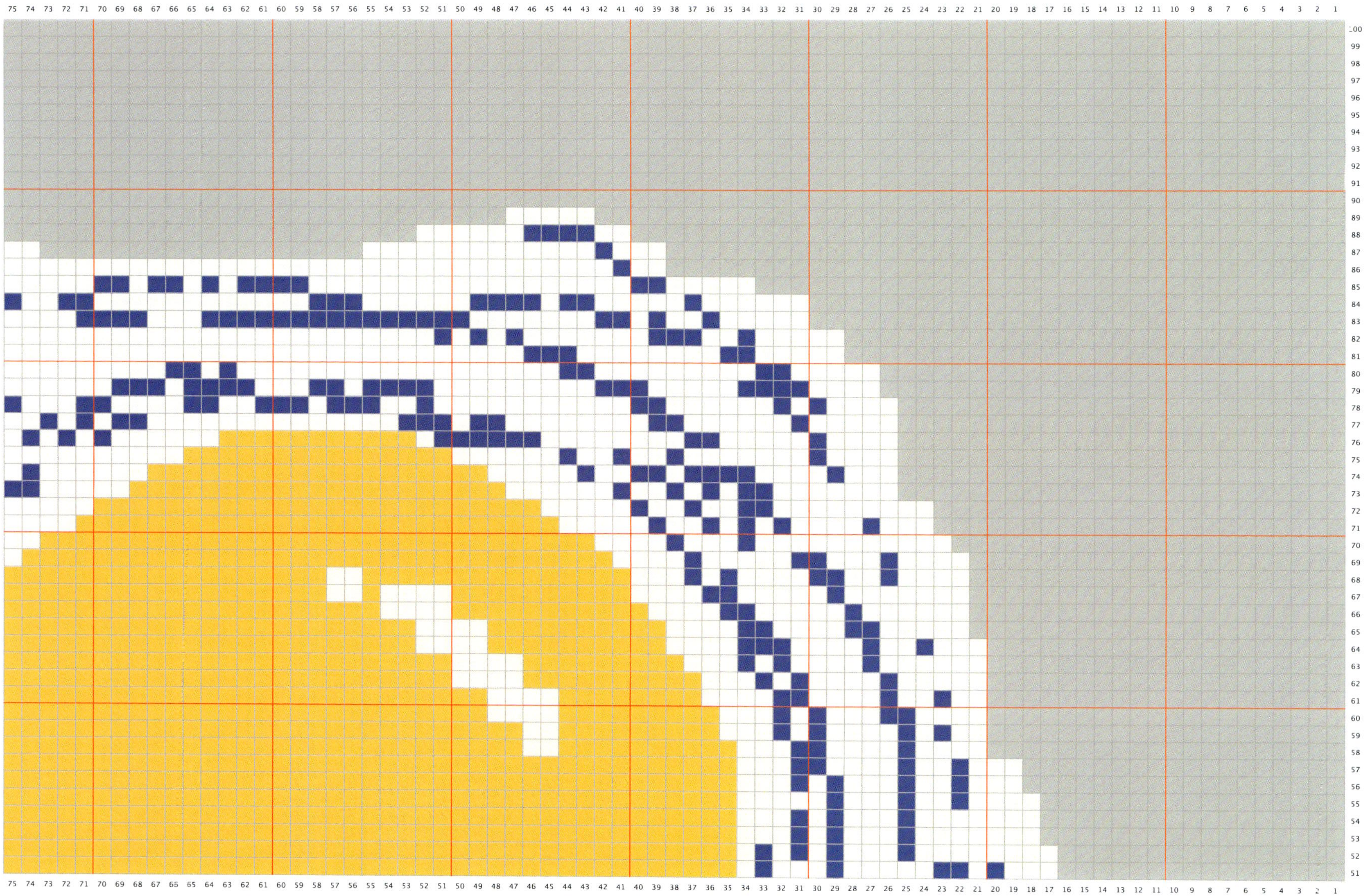

Color Key
One square = one knot

- Royal
- Aran
- Yellow
- No knot

LOWER LEFT

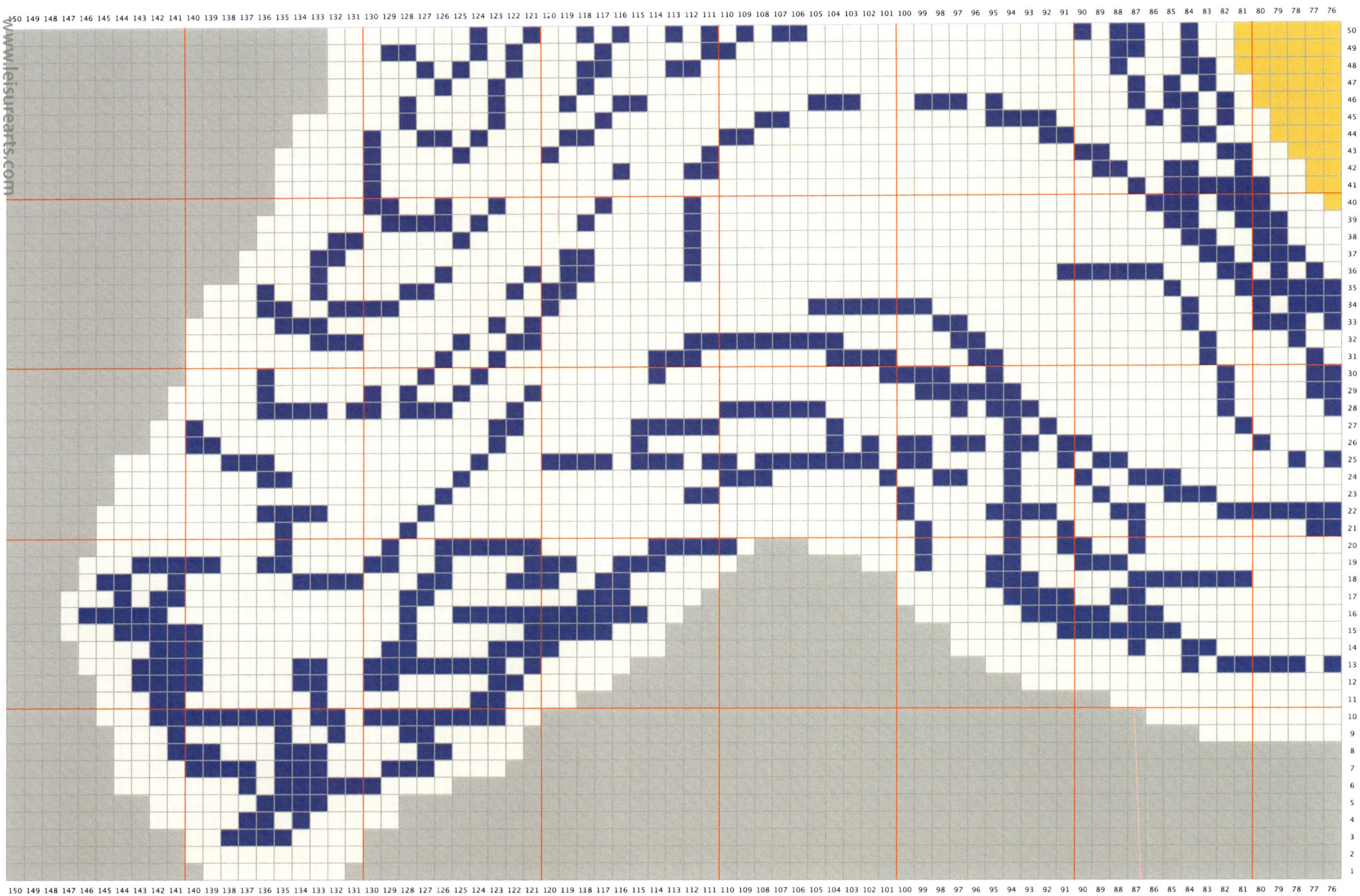

Color Key
One square = one knot

- Royal
- Aran
- Yellow
- No knot

LOWER RIGHT

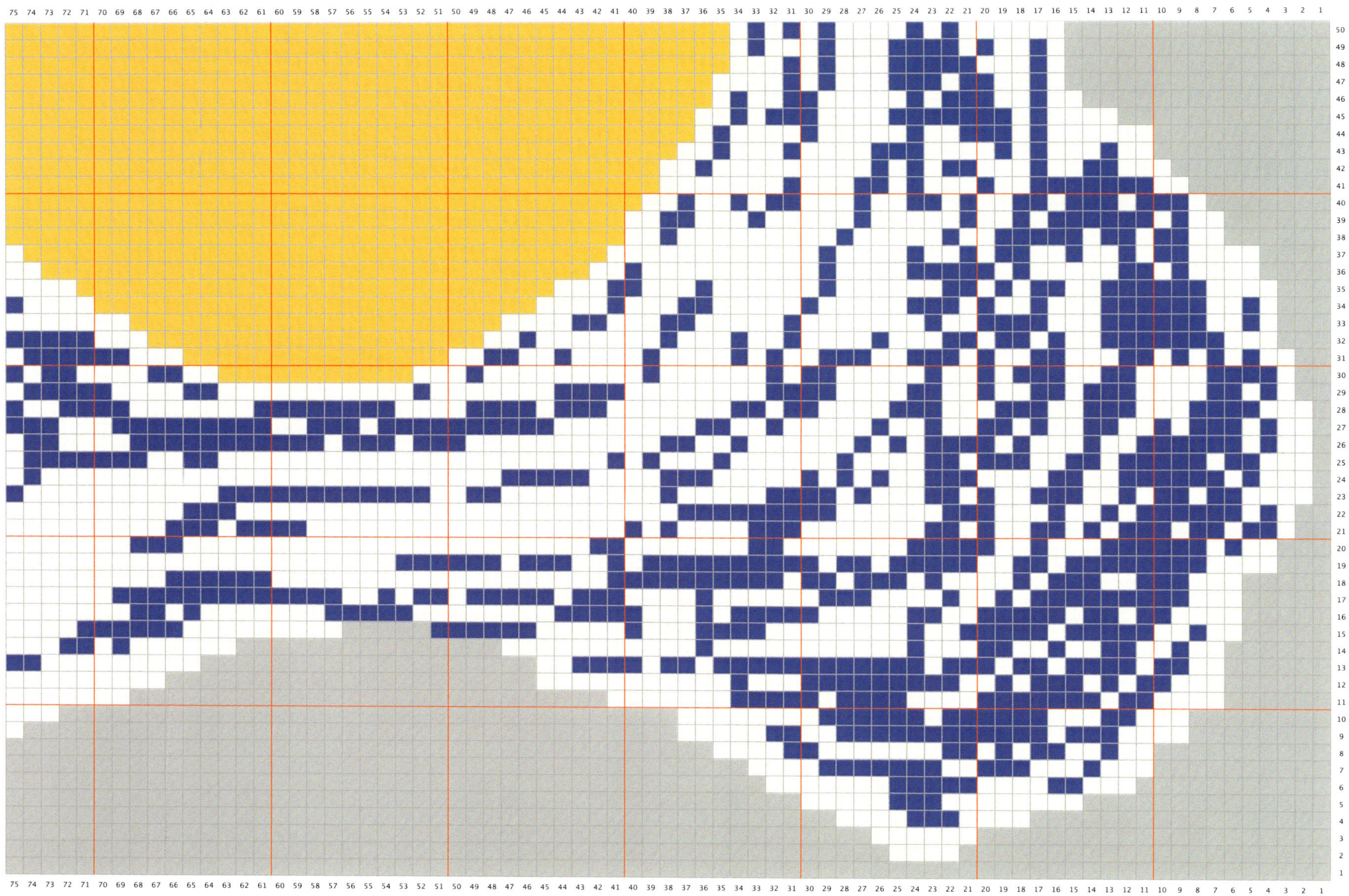

Color Key
One square = one knot

- Royal
- Aran
- Yellow
- No knot

About the Author

Dedication

For Edward.
With you by my side
I can do anything.

Heidi Gustad is an artist and craft project designer, specializing in latch hook, knitting and crochet with a general fondness for needlecrafts. Heidi's aesthetic can best be described as an edgy-meets-homey blend of contemporary and vintage, unapologetically crafted in primary colors. You can read more about Heidi and her work at HandsOccupied.com or by following her on social media @handsoccupied.

Sample Makers

Thank you to my sample makers, without whom this work would not have been possible: Stefanie Goodwin-Ritter, Mariah Somerville, Tommy Schafer, Jackie Valdez, & Marjorie Woolard.

Production Team: Technical Editor—Stephanie Hill; Graphic Designer—Beth Oberholtzer; Photo Stylist—Lori Wenger; Photographer—Jason Masters.

Made in U.S.A.